ON THE RIVER

Written and illustrated by
Lesley Anne Ivory

Burke Books — LONDON & TORONTO

First published April 1976
© Lesley Anne Ivory 1976
All rights reserved. No part of this publication may be reproduced, stored in a retrieval system, or transmitted in any form or by any means, electronic, mechanical, photo-copying, recording or otherwise, without the prior permission of Burke Publishing Company Limited or Burke Publishing (Canada) Limited.

ISBN 0 222 00421 5 Hardbound
ISBN 0 222 00423 1 Limp
ISBN 0 222 00419 3 Library

Burke Publishing Company Limited,
14 John Street, London, WC1N 2EJ.
Burke Publishing (Canada) Limited,
P.O. Box 48 Toronto-Dominion Centre,
Toronto 111, Ontario.

Printed in Great Britain by
William Clowes & Sons Ltd., London & Beccles

A river is starting here.

A little stream comes from the hills.

It gets wider as it goes.

River birds look for fish.

So do fishermen.

Some birds nest on the water.

Animals drink from the water.

Otters love to swim in the river.

The river flows through the country.

Then it flows through a town.

Boats go up and down the river.

It's fun to paddle a canoe on the river.

This river barge is someone's home.

So is this boat.

Traffic goes across the bridge

to the other bank of the river.

The river gets wider

and wider.

Now the river is deep enough

for big ships to sail on it.

At last, the river joins the sea.

GOD'S TRUTH

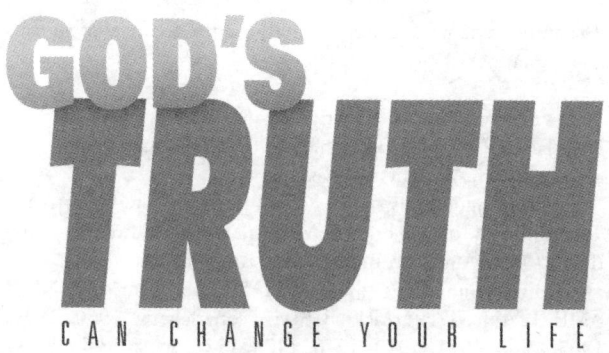

CAN CHANGE YOUR LIFE

GEORGE R. KNIGHT

Nampa, Idaho | www.pacificpress.com

Cover design by Steve Lanto
Cover design resources from iStockphoto.com | 613222434
Inside design by Aaron Troia

Copyright © 2018 by Pacific Press® Publishing Association
Printed in the United States of America
All rights reserved

The author assumes full responsibility for the accuracy of all facts and quotations as cited in this book.

Unless otherwise noted, all Scripture quotations are from the New King James Version®. Copyright © 1982 by Thomas Nelson. Used by permission. All rights reserved.

Scripture quotations marked GNT are from the Good News Translation® (Today's English Version, Second Edition). Copyright © 1992 American Bible Society. All rights reserved.

Scripture quotations marked NASB are from the NEW AMERICAN STANDARD BIBLE®, copyright © 1960, 1962, 1963, 1968, 1971, 1972, 1973, 1975, 1977, 1995 by the Lockman Foundation. Used by permission. www.lockman.org.

Scriptures quotations marked RSV are from the Revised Standard Version of the Bible, copyright © 1946, 1952, 1971 by the Division of Christian Education of the National Council of the Churches of Christ in the U.S.A. Used by permission.

Additional copies of this book are available for purchase by calling toll-free 1-800-765-6955 or by visiting http://www.adventistbookcenter.com.

ISBN 978-0-8163-6498-5

July 2019

All Scripture is inspired by God and is useful for teaching the truth, rebuking error, correcting faults, and giving instruction for right living, so that the person who serves God may be fully qualified and equipped to do every kind of good deed.

—*2 Timothy 3:16, 17, GNT*

Contents

A Word to the Reader	9
1. Good News in a Confusing World	11
2. Jesus: The Center of the Story	16
3. Creation or Evolution?	21
4. What Went Wrong With God's Perfect World?	26
5. God's Solution to the Sin Problem	31
6. Becoming More Like Jesus	36
7. Totally Dedicated to God	41
8. What Is God Like? A Glimpse of His Law	46
9. Christians and God's Law	51
10. A Weekly Gift From Jesus	56
11. Time for Life's Most Important Things	62
12. A Public Testimony of Our Faith	67
13. What Happens When We Die?	72
14. What Is Jesus Doing Now?	78
15. Jesus Hasn't Left Us in the Dark	83
16. God's Last Message to a Dying World	88
17. Judgment Is Good News	94
18. The Hope of the World	99

19. Being Ready to Meet Jesus	104
20. What Happens After Jesus Returns?	110
21. Infinite Hitler or Loving God?	116
22. The Eternal Home of God's Children	122

A Word to the Reader

Truth has come on hard times. Many twenty-first-century people have given up on the idea of universal truth. "You have your truth and I have mine" is the oft-repeated sentiment.

But maybe it is time to take a look at that idea. After all, we all agree that it is not wise for healthy people to step out of ten-story windows. The truth of gravity is a point of agreement. In fact, the entire scientific project, and the technology growing out of it, is based on the proposition that there is truth "out there" waiting to be discovered.

This little book sets forth the idea that there is not only truth in the material realm but also in the social and spiritual, and that this very concept is foundational to health for both individuals and societies. Beyond that, it suggests that God's truth in the Bible, when taken seriously, will transform people's lives by setting them free from destructive attitudes and lifestyles and put them on a path that will enrich their personal and family lives.

God's Truth Can Change Your Life!

Blessings to my readers as you launch out in the search for a truth that can lead to genuine well-being.

George R. Knight

1

Good News in a Confusing World

*Your word is a lamp to guide me
and a light for my path.*
—Psalm 119:105, GNT

Taurus (April 20–May 20): Get everything checked off your list today. You'll feel less like doing it tomorrow. There could be a conflict this evening between you and your mate. . . .

"**Virgo (Aug. 23–Sept. 22):** You need to decide what you want to be, do, and have within five days, five months, and five years. Include your sweetheart or business partner in your discussion and you may get a few more good ideas."

People everywhere are looking for advice and meaning. The fact that nearly every newspaper carries a daily horoscope column testifies to that fact. And if the advice given in the above counsel isn't specific enough, a note following the horoscope provides a phone number that can be contacted for ninety-five cents a minute for personal forecasts.

The search for meaning and guidance
From the beginning of recorded history, people have been seeking advice from astrologers, always with the hope that today will be the day of their "lucky star." But the heavenly bodies were only one place that the ancients looked for meaning and advice. Some examined the livers of sacrificial animals (hepatoscopy) for formations that might reveal hints as to the will of the gods. And other wisdom seekers poured oil into a basin of water and then observed the resulting bubbles and rings in their search for guidance in the affairs of practical life (hydromancy).

Kings of the earth's most powerful nations went to war or stayed at home depending on what readings they found in livers, bubbles, or stars. On a more personal level, individuals decided for or against major business deals or marriages on the strength of such evidence.

But there is a better source for such information than the accidental arrangements of bubbles, stars, or lumps of blood and flesh. That better way is God's revelation in the Bible.

According to Paul, "the sacred writings" found in the Bible "are able to instruct you for salvation through faith in Christ Jesus." "All scripture," he indicates, "is inspired by God and profitable for teaching, for reproof, for correction, and for training in righteousness, that the man of God may be complete, equipped for every good work" (2 Timothy 3:15–17, RSV). And Peter claims that the Bible is as "a light that shines in a dark place" (2 Peter 1:19), while the psalmist proclaims that the Bible "is a lamp to my feet and a light to my path" (Psalm 119:105).

Countless millions of people have found the Bible to be just what it claims to be—a provider of perspective on the meaning of life and a fountainhead of principles for the making of daily decisions.

The purpose of the Bible

The Bible reveals truths that we couldn't possibly know except through God's revelation. Yet it is not an exhaustive source of knowledge. It was never intended to be a "divine encyclopedia" that seeks to answer all our questions. In fact, it leaves most questions unanswered.

On the other hand, the Bible does provide answers to our most basic and most essential questions. As such, the Bible gives answers to life's "big questions": the meaning of life and death, where the world came from, what the future will be, how the problem of sin arose and how it is being dealt with, and so on. Through its teachings on these important issues the Bible provides both a perspective for understanding the universe we live in and principles by which to live our daily lives.

The ultimate authority

We need to remember in our study that the Bible is the ultimate test of Christian truth. Isaiah put it nicely when he wrote: "To the law and to the testimony [the Scriptures of Isaiah's day]! If they do not speak according to this word, it is because there is no light in them" (Isaiah 8:20). Isaiah wrote that counsel about people who claimed to have authoritative knowledge from the supernatural world. He was telling the people of his day that *all such claims to knowledge must be tested against the teaching of the Bible. If such people have true light from God, then their ideas will be in harmony with the teachings of the Bible.*

Isaiah's advice holds true in our day. All too often we bring our ideas to the Bible and find a few passages to support our biases. But such an approach is wrongheaded. We need to get our ideas of spiritual realities and truths from Bible study rather than imposing our views onto God's Word.

That approach is true for both individuals and churches. Some churches and pastors claim to be the only authoritative interpreters of God's Word. Such people and religious bodies at times even teach things contrary to the Bible.

Such claims are out of harmony with the intent of the Bible. According to Isaiah, it is the Bible that is the ultimate authority, not churches, pastors, friends, or family. The Bible is not to be tested by their ideas but their ideas by the Bible.

Those who desire to be faithful to the teachings of the Bible need to go straight to the source of truth. It is from the Bible itself that we discover if a church or a pastor or a book is on the right track. The Bible as God's Word is the ultimate authority in all spiritual matters. We need to thank God daily for the certainties of His Word.

Good news for today
We can thank God for the Bible as we seek answers to the meaning of life. This chapter is the first of twenty-two that will explore what the Bible says about a variety of themes, including what went wrong with God's perfect world, why our lives are too often lived in frustration, what Jesus is doing now, when He will come again, the nature of heaven and hell, and a host of others. But central to our explorations will be Jesus and God's plan for each of us to live fuller lives both in this life and for eternity. Truly the Bible's answers provide good news for a confusing world.

2

Jesus: The Center of the Story

For God loved the world so much that he gave his only Son, so that everyone who believes in him may not die but have eternal life.
—John 3:16, GNT

You don't have to be a Christian to know that there is something special about Jesus. After all, even the dating system upon which our calendars are based is divided between B.C. (before Christ) and A.D. (*anno Domini*, Latin for "in the year of our Lord"). No wonder Jesus has been called the hinge of history. Our very understanding of history puts Jesus at the center.

The same picture is found in the Bible. The Old Testament points forward to Jesus as the Lamb of God who will take away the sins of the world. And the New Testament looks back on His life, death, and the church He founded to take His teachings to the far corners of the earth. Thus Jesus is not only the focal point of history but also the very center of the Bible story.

Jesus: The Center of the Story

Who is Jesus?

But we need to ask, What does the Bible teach us about Jesus? One thing that it tells us is that Jesus is a unique individual and that there has been no one like Him in the history of the world.

How is that? you may be thinking. The Bible's answer is that He is both divine and human. Thus the apostle John tells us that "in the beginning was the Word, and the Word was with God, and the Word was God" (John 1:1). John continues on to tell us that "the Word became flesh and dwelt among us" (verse 14). That Word is none other than Jesus.

The Gospel of Matthew is even more specific about the person of Jesus. " 'Behold,' " we read, " 'the virgin shall be with child, and bear a Son, and they shall call His name Immanuel,' which is translated, 'God with us' " (Matthew 1:23). That Son, of course, was Jesus Christ, born of the virgin Mary and the Holy Spirit (verse 18).

In summary, Jesus is not only the center of the Bible and history, but He is also a bridge between God the Father and the human race. His unique divine-human nature did not come about by accident. That thought brings us to the question of why Jesus became human; a topic on which the Bible is very clear.

What is the work of Jesus?

Perhaps the best place to begin is with John 3:16,

which is many people's favorite Bible verse: "For God so loved the world that He gave His only begotten Son, that whoever believes in Him should not perish but have everlasting life." There are several things that we should note about that verse. The first is that God is not against people who have sinned and messed up their lives. To the contrary, He loved them so much that He sent Jesus to rescue them from the mess that we call earthly history. A second point that John 3:16 highlights is that without God's sending of Jesus, Earth and its inhabitants would eventually "perish" or self-destruct. That threat brings us to the verse's third point—that God sent Jesus to planet Earth on a rescue mission. The Bible pictures Jesus as the very center point between destruction and salvation and healing.

Matthew's Gospel makes that point extremely clear when it claims that Jesus was sent to "save His people from their sins" (Matthew 1:21). There is an interesting thought. Modern people want to be saved from poverty and disease, while the Jews of Jesus' day wanted to be saved from their hated Roman rulers. Most of us would like that kind of a savior—one that could give us all the earthly freedom and money and food that we could want. But the Bible tells us that Jesus had a more important mission—to save us from the sins that destroy our lives and that will eventually reap the "wages" of eternal death (Romans 6:23).

As a result, Jesus' mission to Earth was the most

important event in our history. That thought brings us to the word *Christ*. We tend to think of Christ as Jesus' last name. But that is not what the word implies. His earthly name was Jesus of Nazareth or Jesus, son of Joseph, rather than Jesus Christ.

Here is an important point. *Christ* is the Greek word for the Hebrew term *Messiah*. Both of them mean the "anointed one"—the one who has a special mission. Thus Jesus is called the Christ because He was sent by God the Father to rescue the human race from disaster. As a result, we find that Jesus is not only the center of history and the Bible, but He is also the center of God's plan for saving you and me.

That thought brings us to another special Bible word—*gospel*. *Gospel* means "good news." As such, the gospel is the good news that Jesus has come to Earth to rescue us.

And how did He accomplish His rescue mission? The Bible explains His task in several steps. First, Jesus in His earthly existence lived a life totally free from sin. Thus He was qualified to be the sinless "Lamb of God" who could take away "the sin of the world" (John 1:29).

The second step was Jesus' death on the cross for our sins (1 Corinthians 15:3; Galatians 3:10–13). But we all know that a dead Savior doesn't do us any good. As a result, Paul tells us that the good news is that not only did Jesus die for us; but that He also obtained the victory over death through His resurrection from the grave (1 Corinthians 15:4). The really good news is that Jesus accomplished those things for us so that we can share His victory. Thus He tells us that "I am He who lives, and was dead, and behold, I am alive forevermore. . . . And I have the keys of Hades [the grave] and of Death" (Revelation 1:18).

Jesus needs to be the center of my story

Jesus is truly the center of history, the Bible, and God's rescue plan. But those facts will do us absolutely no good unless we make Him the very center of our lives. The most important thing that you and I can do today and every day is to invite the Jesus of the Bible into our lives and make a decision to live a life that follows Him as both our Lord and Savior.

3

Creation or Evolution?

*In the beginning God created
the heavens and the earth.*

—Genesis 1:1

I don't have enough faith to be an atheist. And I never did. For the first nineteen years of my life, I was not a Christian or a believer in any religion.

My teachers tried to explain how things just happened throughout ceaseless ages of evolution. But even as a teenager, I knew that something does not come out of nothing, that intelligence does not flow out of ignorance, and that order is not the child of chaos. *I might have been gullible about some things, but I was not that gullible.* Let's take a brief look at some of the issues.

The problem of chance

Let's first look at the chance theory. The mathematical odds are against such a happening. That is illustrated by Dr. A. Cressy Morrison, a former president of the New York Academy of Sciences, in *Seven Reasons Why a Scientist Believes in God.* Dr. Morrison says:

> Let me begin by supposing you mark ten pennies from one to ten, put them in your pocket, and give them a good shake. Now try to draw them out in sequence from one to ten, putting each coin back in your pocket after each draw and shuffling them all again. Mathematically, your chance of drawing number one first is one in ten; of drawing one and two in succession, one in 100; of drawing the first three numbers in succession, one in 1,000. The chance that you might draw all of them, from number one through number ten, in that order, would reach the unbelievable figure of one in 10,000,000,000.[1]

If the element of chance is that great for a problem with ten factors, you can begin to grasp the implications involved in the evolution of the universe or of even the simplest living organism, which is thousands of times more complex than your family automobile.

A businessman once had an interesting common-sense insight into the whole problem of the chance theory:

> It takes a girl in our factory about two days to learn how to put the 17 parts of a meat chopper together. It may be that these millions of worlds each with its separate orbit, all balanced so wonderfully in

space—it may be that they just happened.

"It may be that by a billion years of tumbling about they finally arranged themselves. I don't know, I am merely a plain manufacturer of cutlery. But this I do know, that you can shake the 17 parts of a meat chopper around in a washtub for the next 17 billion years and you'll never have a meat chopper."[2]

Even if people are willing to believe in the odds of the accidental evolution of an infinite and orderly universe, they are still stuck with a bedrock question—where did the raw material and/or energy come from in the first place?

It is evident that it takes a great deal of faith to accept the chance theory, which is apparently built upon the belief that time, in itself, is a creative agent.

The Bible's answer

Now let's look briefly at the Creation theory. It seems that a study of the heavens and the natural world has always tended to make believers out of people because here they come face to face with infinity in time, space, and complexity, which they can both see and test. The ancients had a saying that "the undevout astronomer is mad." And Alfred Noyes, in a poem about Isaac Newton, one of the world's greatest minds, said: "The universe exists, and by that one impossible fact declares itself a miracle, postulates an infinite power."[3]

The Bible teaches the issue head on with no apologies in its very first words. "In the beginning," we read, "God created the heavens and the earth" (Genesis 1:1).

The Genesis account of the creation of the world adds several more important facts about Creation. One is that all Three Persons of the Trinity were involved in the process. That thought is reflected in Genesis 1:26, "Let *Us* make man in *Our* image" (emphasis added). The "Us" is the same as the Father, Son, and Holy Spirit of Matthew 28:19. Thus we find the Spirit (Genesis 1:2) and the Son (John 1:3) working with the Father in the act of creation.

The Bible doesn't tell us how God created the world. But it does declare that "by the word of the Lord the heavens were made, and all the host of them by the breath of His mouth. . . . He spoke, and it was done; He commanded, and it stood fast" (Psalm 33:6, 9). And the book of Hebrews notes that "by faith we understand that the worlds were framed by the word of God, so that the things which are seen were not made of things which are visible" (Hebrews 11:3).

To be honest, we probably don't want to be too close to that kind of power, even if we could understand it. Some years ago I had a slight glimpse of that kind of power when I stood at ground zero in Hiroshima, above which the world's first atomic bomb detonated and destroyed this major city and countless lives in one mighty flash. *If the unlocking of one atomic chain could do that kind of damage,* I remember thinking, *I don't want to be anywhere near the kind of power it took to create the entire world and all it contains.*

Remembering God's creative act

While we cannot understand God's creative act, we have been commanded to remember it. "Remember the Sabbath day," God tells us in the heart of the Ten Commandments, "to keep it holy." Why? "For in six days the Lord made the heavens and the earth, the sea, and all that is in them, and rested the seventh day. Therefore the Lord blessed the Sabbath day and hallowed it" (Exodus 20:8, 11). Some people seem to think that this command is for the Jews, but the Bible plainly teaches that the Sabbath was given to humans at the end of Creation week (Genesis 2:1–3), thousands of years before there were any Jews. Beyond that, the command is resurrected in Revelation 14:7, right before the second coming of Jesus (verses 14–20).

It is one of the strange facts of history that the one commandment that says "remember" is the one most people forget. But God gave it for a reason. He wants us to remember who He is as Creator every Sabbath.

---

1. A. Cressy Morrison, *Seven Reasons Why a Scientist Believes in God* (Westwood, NJ: Fleming H. Revell, 1962), 12.

2. "God as a Personality," *Awake!*, April 8, 1979, 4–8.

3. Alfred Noyes, *Newton*, in *The Torch-Bearers*, vol. 1, *Watchers of the Sky* (New York: Frederick A. Stokes, 1922), 226.

4

What Went Wrong With God's Perfect World?

"From your heart come the evil ideas which lead you to kill, commit adultery, and do other immoral things; to rob, lie, and slander others."
—Matthew 15:19, GNT

You don't have to be real smart to know that something is wrong with the world. Just turn on the television or read the newspaper. War, natural disasters, and political intrigue are news on the global level, while divorce, financial corruption, murder, and sexual infidelity are reported of individuals.

God may have created a perfect world and declared that it was "very good" (Genesis 1:31), but the one we live in is messed up. We are made for life but end up with death. We are made for happiness but all too often are faced by disappointment and misery. "What," our hearts and minds cry out, "went wrong? How did we get into this mess?"

What Went Wrong With God's Perfect World?

The Bible's answer

The Bible tells us that things began to go wrong when Earth's first human beings (Adam and Eve) decided to disobey God and do things their own way (Genesis 3:1–6). God hadn't required all that much of them, but they thought they were smarter than He was and didn't need His guidance. They decided to live life their way and by their principles rather than His.

The result was absolute disaster. It would have been bad enough if Earth's first parents had gone off the track themselves, but the problem spread to their children. Thus we find in Genesis 4 their son Cain murdering his brother Abel. A moral disease had been let loose, and the results are reflected not only in the Bible but throughout human history, as brother rises against brother and nations struggle among themselves for power, territory, and wealth.

The sad truth is that no matter how ignorant people are, they always know how to sin. In fact, that is the one thing we don't have to teach children. The Bible reflects upon the universality of sin when it declares that sin passed from Adam and Eve to all their descendants (Romans 5:12–19) and "all have sinned and fall short of the glory of God" (Romans 3:23).

The nature of sin

But we must ask, What is sin? Here is a point at which most people are confused. They think of sin as an action, something we do—like murder, stealing, or worshiping an idol. I would like to suggest that such actions are the symptoms of sin rather than the core of the problem.

The origin of sin with Eve in the Garden of Eden illustrates that point. Most people believe that she sinned when she took and ate the forbidden fruit. They are dead wrong. Think about it for a moment, and you will see the point. After all, before she took the fruit, something happened in her heart and mind. Before she took the fruit, she had to put herself in the place of God; she had to choose her authority over His; she had to place her will above God's will. In essence, she had to place herself at the center of her life, in effect becoming the god of her life. Eve sinned when she rebelled against God and chose her own will instead of God's. Out of that rebellion flowed sinful actions.

Thus we can think of sin as having at least two levels. The first is SIN, or rebellion against God and the choice to do our will rather than His. The second level is represented by sinful actions in daily life that we might think of as sins. Jesus captured that fact in Matthew 15:18, 19 when He pointed out that such evil actions as murder and adultery flow out of the heart or mind. With that in mind, we can portray the sin problem as follows:

$$SIN \rightarrow sins$$

In summary, rebellion in the heart leads to sinful actions and a sinful way of life.

The root of sin is loving oneself more than God and other people. Thus if I love myself more than God, I will be tempted to break His commandments, dishonor His name, and desecrate His holy day. Again, if I love myself more than other people, I will be tempted to steal their things, use their bodies, or take their lives. And with those dynamics, we come to the problems that we face daily in a world that has gone wrong—that has rebelled against the will and ways of God.

The results of sin

Sin has had many results. Genesis 3 points out that the first was a separation between Adam and Eve and God. They felt a guilt that the Bible refers to as nakedness and that made God's presence unbearable. Where once they loved to be with God, now they hid from Him and even feared Him (verses 7–10).

A second result of sin was that people became alienated from one another. Adam and Eve had had Earth's only perfect marriage; but once sin came in, they began to blame each other for their problems. Adam was quite sure that Eve was the source of their problem, and she undoubtedly felt the same toward him (verses 11, 12). Those dynamics are still with us in the twenty-first century. Sin has disrupted all our social relationships.

A third result of sin is that it affects each person's relationship with his or her own "self." In Genesis 3:13, when God asked Eve what the problem was, her reply was that it wasn't her fault; the devil had made her do it. Here we come face to face with the problem of people being unwilling and, in many cases, unable to face up to and correctly evaluate their personal responsibility in making choices.

A fourth result of sin is death (Genesis 3:19). Paul graphically highlights that point when he writes that "the wages of sin is death" (Romans 6:23).

The need for healing
Because of sin, we live in a sick world that desperately needs healing in terms of our relationship to God, to other people, to our own selves, and to the world around us. It is to this topic that we will turn in our next segment of exploring what the Bible teaches.

5

God's Solution to the Sin Problem

For it is by God's grace that you have been saved through faith. It is not the result of your own efforts, but God's gift.
—Ephesians 2:8, 9, GNT

The most important thing to know about sin and its results is that human beings can't solve the problem. Try as hard as we will, at the end of the day, we are as messed up as ever. Of course, we do manage to improve on some things, but that only tempts us to be proud of our goodness and to feel that we are better than other people. Such is the sin of the Pharisee—the "good" person, who most of us find to be totally obnoxious.

The uniqueness of Christianity
All religions and philosophies are concerned with the problem of evil and with making people better. Reform your life, become enlightened, improve your social

skills, overcome sinful habits, and the like is the wisdom of the ages. And yet at the end of people's lives, they are still far short of the goal.

Maybe, think some, we need longer to overcome the effects of sin and selfishness. Life just isn't long enough to overcome all our faults. To get around that difficulty, some religious groups have invented the theory of reincarnation. If you can't do it in one life, the theory goes, you could certainly get your act together if you had a hundred or thousand sequential lives to accomplish the task. That must certainly be the answer.

Wrong! Time is not the problem. Rather, it is the condition of the human heart and mind. The prophet Jeremiah is right on target when he writes that "the heart is deceitful above all things, and desperately wicked" (Jeremiah 17:9). In another place, he asks, "Can the Ethiopian change his skin or the leopard its spots?" (Jeremiah 13:23). It is just as impossible for humans to do good when we are accustomed to doing evil. The bad news is that humans cannot of themselves climb out of the pit of sin with all its ego-centered selfishness.

That is where Christianity is unique among the world's religions and philosophies. Whereas all other approaches center on human achievement in one way or another, Christianity recognizes right up front that humans can never conquer sin and evil.

Rather, the Bible tells us, God points out human

inadequacy and takes the initiative by developing a plan to rescue humans from their plight.

The Christian answer

At the very center of the Christian faith is the fact that salvation begins with God in His gift of Jesus. "For God so loved the world," the Bible tells us, "that he gave his only Son, that whoever believes in him should not perish but have eternal life" (John 3:16, RSV).

The good news is that God is not out to condemn and destroy sinners, but rather to help them in every possible way. Thus Jesus was sent to become "the Lamb of God who takes away the sin of the world" (John 1:29). And with those truths in mind, we have come to the centrality of the cross. In short, Jesus died in our place that we might have life.

One author makes that point exceptionally clear, writing that "Christ was treated as we deserve, that we might be treated as He deserves. He was condemned for our sins, in which He had no share, that we might be justified by His righteousness, in which we had no share. He suffered the death which was ours, that we might receive the life which was His."[1]

The means by which God provides the possibility of salvation from sin is called *grace* in the Bible. The word *grace* is closely related to the word *gift*. Grace is God's gift of salvation to helpless humans. Through grace God does for us what we cannot do for ourselves. As a result, Paul writes that "by grace you have been saved through faith, and that [is] not of yourselves; it is the gift of God, not of works, lest anyone should boast" (Ephesians 2:8, 9). The absolutely unique element of Christianity among the world's religions is salvation by grace on the basis of Christ's sacrificial, substitutionary death on the cross.

While the *bad news* is that humans are hopelessly lost in sin, the *good news* (gospel) is "that Christ died for our sins . . . , and that He rose again" (1 Corinthians 15:3, 4).

The human part in salvation

Humans, we need to repeat, can do nothing to save themselves. Our part is not doing but accepting God's gift in Christ. Each individual must accept the grace gift personally. But even that choice is only possible because God's Spirit gives us faith and empowers us to say yes to God. Salvation is totally by grace alone and accepted through faith alone.

We have arrived at an important point in our discussion. A person can choose either to accept or to reject God's great gift. That is why John 3:16 talks about the gift of eternal life for those who believe and Ephesians 2:8 speaks of being saved by grace "through faith." God gives us the opportunity to choose Him. He forces salvation on no one.

But when we do choose Him, He adopts us into His

God's Solution to the Sin Problem

family (Romans 8:14–17; John 1:12, 13) and forgives our sins. The good news is that "if we confess our sins, He is faithful and just to forgive us our sins and to cleanse us from all unrighteousness" (1 John 1:9).

That forgiveness and cleansing is the beginning of the Christian life. But please remember that it is God in His grace who does the forgiving and cleansing. And at the same time, He does something else—He enables us to be born again by the Holy Spirit (John 3:3, 5, 7) and makes us new creatures in Christ (2 Corinthians 5:17).

As a result, Christians receive not only the blessing of forgiveness but also new hearts and minds. It is significant that Jesus and the New Testament authors never talk of becoming a Christian in terms of becoming better and better. Rather, the process is described as a death and crucifixion and a resurrection to a new way of life (Romans 6:2–8). It is that new way of life that we will examine in the next segment in our survey of the Bible's major teachings.

---

1. Ellen G. White, *The Desire of Ages* (Mountain View, CA: Pacific Press®, 1898), 25.

6

Becoming More Like Jesus

*Christ also suffered for us, leaving us an example,
that you should follow His steps.*
—1 Peter 2:21

Some years ago I had an Islamic student from an Arab nation taking my course in philosophy. About halfway through the course, he asked me if I could take him to the bookstore to help him buy a Bible. Then a month later, he surprised me by stopping by my office to discuss his first ever visit to a Christian church of any type. Two men, he told me, stood in front of the church, and one put the other under water. Then, my student noted, the first man told the one who had been under the water that he was a "new creature," a "new man."

An important point

"I looked very carefully at that man," said the student, "but he wasn't a new creature at all. He was the same man who had been submerged in water. Please help me understand what happened."

His questioning shock provided me the opportunity to give my Islamic friend a Bible study on baptism. But more importantly, he had enabled me to grasp a crucial lesson about Christianity. He helped me see a point that we too often miss; namely, that at our conversion, the Bible tells us that we have a new heart and mind. While that is good and true, it is just as true that we come out of the watery grave of baptism with the same old body with all its maladjusted habits and appetites.

Thus it is that we enter the Christian life thinking we will live the life of victory from there on out. But the next day we find ourselves falling for the same old temptations, and we realize that God's work with us isn't finished just because we have been baptized and joined the church. In fact, in many ways He is just beginning His work in our lives.

The dynamics of the Christian journey

The good news for new Christians who have fallen flat on their faces and sinned is that God is ever ready to forgive when we come to Him in prayer, asking for pardon. It is always true that "if we confess our sins, He is faithful and just to forgive us our sins" (1 John 1:9). We do not need to fear. There is no way that we can exhaust the vast reservoir of His grace. He always forgives the repentant sinner.

But the Bible makes it plain that there is more to the Christian life than forgiveness. Paul points out that just as people are buried like Christ in the watery grave of baptism, so they are resurrected like Him to a new way of life. "Even so," he writes, the Christian "also should walk in newness of life" (Romans 6:4).

Of course, it is impossible for us to "walk" or live the Christian life in our own power. As a result, God provides the empowering grace of the Holy Spirit. Christians are never left alone to struggle through life. To the contrary, God's Spirit is there to enable each Christian at every step. And when we fall back into some of our old habits, He is more than willing to forgive us when we see our mistakes and ask Him to do so.

The Christian's life can be defined as a walk with God. That walk has two distinct elements: both of which are called *sanctification*. The first aspect of sanctification comes from the meaning of the word itself, which is "to be set apart for holy use." As a result, at conversion every Christian is set apart by God for holiness. The meaning of the word *holy*, it should be pointed out, is to be different. And just as God and His ways are different from those of a sinful world, so are His children to live lives governed by a different set of values than they did before they became Christians.

That thought brings us to the second aspect of sanctification—walking with God on a daily basis and becoming progressively more like Him in character.

Becoming More Like Jesus

From the Bible's perspective, a person will either walk in the way of the world or walk in the way of God. But no person can follow both paths at the same time. It is up to each of us as to which one will be ours.

The Bible is quite clear that the two walks have two quite different destinations (Romans 6:16–23). Jesus made that point explicit when He told His followers to "enter by the narrow gate; for wide is the gate and broad is the way that leads to destruction, and there are many who go in by it. Because narrow is the gate and difficult is the way which leads to life, and there are few who find it" (Matthew 7:13, 14).

The good news is that born-again Christians have found the correct path. Their challenge after baptism is to follow that path. And while that task is impossible for the unconverted, Jesus tells His followers that with His enabling power the path of life is the easier one. "Come to Me, all you who labor and are heavy laden, and I will give you rest. Take My yoke upon you and learn from Me, for I am gentle and lowly in heart, and you will find rest for your souls. For My yoke is easy and My burden is light" (Matthew 11:28–30).

Imitating Jesus

The real challenge in the Christian life is not working to improve under our own power, but to stay on the right path and to stay yoked up or connected to Christ who knows the way and can provide us with daily strength for life's journey. The long run will demonstrate that it is the way of the sinner that is the most difficult as the sinner's life is beset with problems brought on by selfishness and intemperate living.

One path leads individuals to become more and more like the devil. The other leads them to become progressively more like Jesus and that God who is "love" by definition (1 John 4:8).

While we may be the same people when we rise from the baptismal waters, the best of news is that God wants to take our lives and empower us to become more like Jesus every day.

7

Totally Dedicated to God

*Therefore, whether you eat or drink,
or whatever you do, do all to the glory of God.*
—1 Corinthians 10:31

"**Steward**: One who acts as a supervisor or administrator, as of finances and property, for another or others." Such is the dictionary definition of an important word.

God's managers

When most people hear the word *stewardship*, the first thing that comes to their minds is financial giving. But stewardship is much more than that. While it includes how we handle our finances, stewardship means carefully managing all that God has given us. We are God's stewards in every part of our lives.

One of the important teachings of Jesus is the parable of the talents. In that story, Jesus teaches that God has given each person at least one gift to use for His kingdom. The interesting thing about those gifts is that not everybody gets the same number. We see that in our daily lives. There are some people who seem to be good at everything. But the Bible teaches that those skills are not something they developed on their own but are gifts of God.

In a perfect world, everyone would use their gifts to bless others and glorify their Maker. But all too often people pervert God's gifts and utilize them for selfish purposes. That is where Christianity makes a difference. People who have a saving relationship with God through Jesus dedicate all they own, all they do, and even their entire being to the Lord who has given them everything.

The good news about the parable of the talents in Matthew 25:14–30 is that God doesn't expect equal accomplishments from each of us. That would be both unjust and unfair. After all, the person who has only one talent can never accomplish the same amount as a person gifted with five or six. What God expects, Jesus tells us, is not equal accomplishment but equal dedication. Part of the good news taught in the parable of the talents is that there is a blessing in the use of each one. This chapter will examine two areas of stewardship—our health and our finances.

Dedicated to a healthier life

No one likes being sick. In fact, we hate it. Illness affects every part of our lives. Our bodies ache and hurt, our thinking is clouded, and our personalities all too often express themselves in grumpiness. We soon discover that nothing has any joy or value when we are sick.

But God's will for us is just the opposite. He wants us to be as healthy and happy as possible.

The biblical basis for living a healthy life is found in 1 Corinthians 6, in which Paul tells us that our "body is the temple of the Holy Spirit who is in you, . . . you are not your own. . . . You were bought at a price; therefore glorify God in your body and in your spirit, which are God's" (verses 19, 20).

Wow! There is something that most people never think of. Even our bodies belong to God. And since stewardship means managing God's property, part of Christian stewardship is taking care of our health. Just as we don't like people to destroy our property, so God doesn't want us to pursue lifestyle activities that tear down our physical, mental, and spiritual health.

The biblical idea is that "whether you eat or drink, or whatever you do, do all to the glory of God" (1 Corinthians 10:31). The opposite of that ideal was expressed by Jesus when He said, "Take heed to yourselves, lest your hearts be weighed down with carousing, drunkenness, and cares of this life, and that Day [the second coming of Jesus] come on you unexpectedly" (Luke 21:34).

There is a blessing in good health. And God wants us to be as healthy as possible so that we can be as happy as possible in order to be a blessing to both ourselves and to those around us.

Dedicated to caring for God's finances
The basis for financial stewardship is found in John 3:16, "For God so loved the world that He *gave* His only begotten Son, that whoever believes in Him should not perish but have everlasting life" (emphasis added). God is a giver. And in Jesus, He gave the greatest gift possible.

The Bible's teaching on financial stewardship is based on the fact that God wants us to be like Him in every way. But our giving will always be different from His because everything on Earth belongs to God (Psalm 24:1, 2), even those possessions that He has loaned to us so that we can manage them for Him.

Thus it is that the Bible teaches that Christians are to be responsible to God in their financial lives. Scripture is clear on the fact that most of the money and possessions that God has provided people should be managed responsibly in their daily lives. After all, we all need food and a house, and our children need to be educated to develop their talents for service.

But the Bible is also quite clear that a Christian's financial stewardship includes gifts to God for His gospel work here on Earth. Malachi speaks to that point when he writes: " 'Bring all the tithes into the storehouse . . . , and try [test] Me now in this,' says the

LORD of hosts, 'if I will not open for you the windows of heaven and pour out for you such blessing that there will not be room enough to receive it' " (Malachi 3:10).

Several ideas in that passage should be noted. The first is that God tells us that it is robbery if we fail to be faithful in our tithes and offerings (verse 9). Please note that tithes and offerings are two kinds of financial contributions. In the Bible, the *tithe* (one-tenth of our earnings) always belongs to God. Thus we *return* the tithe that is already His, but we *give* other offerings as God has blessed us in material things.

The good news about financial stewardship is that in giving we actually receive more than we give: God will pour out a blessing on us greater than we can ever imagine.

The Bible teaches us that there is a blessing in every form of Christian stewardship. Taking care of our bodies leads to health and happiness. And financial faithfulness leads to untold blessing. With such promises from God available, each of us needs to decide today to become faithful stewards for God.

8

What Is God Like?
A Glimpse of His Law

*Dear friends, let us love one another,
because love comes from God.
Whoever loves is a child of God and knows God.
Whoever does not love does not know God,
for God is love.*
—1 John 4:7, 8, GNT

Have you ever tried to wash your face by rubbing a mirror on it?

What a stupid question. Mirrors may be useful in discovering that you have egg on your face, but they are not much good for cleaning it.

God's law, James tells us, is like a mirror (James 1:25). It is good for some things but not for others. Paul makes the same point when he writes that "the law is good if one uses it lawfully" (1 Timothy 1:8). Foundational to the lawful use of the law is understanding the nature of God's law.

The real law and God's character

When most people think of biblical law, they think of the Ten Commandments. According to Jesus, that answer is wrong. When asked about the essence of the law, He replied that " 'you shall love the LORD your God with all your heart, with all your soul, and with all your mind.' This is the first and great commandment. And the second is like it: 'You shall love your neighbor as yourself' " (Matthew 22:37–39).

That statement is without doubt the most important one ever made about God's law. Its importance centers on two points. First, it relates the central characteristic of the law to God. First John 4:8 tells us that "God is love." Thus if Christians desire to be like God, they need to be in harmony with His law of love.

A second point implied in Jesus' statement is that a person can keep the many laws of God while at the same time failing in keeping the LAW of God. That fact explains why some people who are very meticulous about obeying the Ten Commandments can be as mean as the devil.

Such people have it all backwards. The thing of most importance is getting our hearts transformed from their natural self-centeredness and self-love to a caring love toward both God and other people. Here is biblical conversion at its deepest level. It is only after our hearts have been converted and transformed at their deepest level by the Holy Spirit that Christians can even begin to think about truly obeying God's many laws.

The relationship between God's LAW and His laws

We have discovered a crucial Bible teaching regarding the law of God; namely, that God's LAW of love is more basic than His many laws. All too many miss the point when they try to keep the laws without having His LAW in their hearts. That makes for some very unloving church members who think they are being faithful to God. They couldn't be more wrong. That is just where the devil wants them.

The proper order is the one taught by Jesus in Matthew 22. His way of looking at the law can be illustrated as follows:

$$LAW \rightarrow laws$$

What that means in daily life is that people who have the LAW of love in their hearts will naturally obey God's many laws.

That is the exact picture that Paul highlights in his letters. In Romans 13:8–10, for example, he explicitly relates the LAW to the laws of the Ten Commandments when he writes that "the commandments, 'You shall not commit adultery,' 'You shall not murder,' 'You shall not steal,' 'You shall not bear false witness,'

'You shall not covet,' and if there is any other commandment, are all summed up in this saying, namely, 'You shall love your neighbor as yourself.'. . . Therefore love is the fulfillment of the law."

Paul in that passage connects the Ten Commandments to the LAW of love. As a result, Jesus' first great commandment of love to God finds expression in the first four commandments of the Decalogue, while its last six commandments flow out of and are built upon loving one's neighbor, which is Christ's second great commandment. Thus if I truly love God, I will not desire to use His name in vain, worship an idol, or break His Sabbath. Likewise, if I truly love God, I will love other people. Thus I will not steal their things, take their lives, and so on.

In short, all Christian law keeping is based on love. And keeping God's law in the spirit of love makes us more like Him, whose defining characteristic is love. In that light, the process of sanctification is the process of becoming more loving, more like Jesus.

The purpose of the law

We noted above that Paul claims that "the law is good if one uses it lawfully" (1 Timothy 1:8). Since that is true, we had better discover the nature of the proper use of the law. But first we need to examine one popular unlawful use of the law. Paul emphasizes it when he writes that "by the deeds of the law no flesh will be justified [or counted righteous or made righteous] in His sight" (Romans 3:20).

The law is good for many things, but it is not the way to salvation. It is not a ladder to heaven. Trying to use the law in that way is like rubbing a mirror on your face to get it clean. Bad move! The function of the mirror is to point out the food on your face so that you can get a washcloth, soap, and water.

That illustration directs us to the true, lawful functions of the law. We will examine its three foremost tasks. First, the law teaches God's ideal for His followers. He desires them not to injure one another, to put Him first in everything, not to lust after the property of others, and so on.

Unfortunately, however, even true Christians fail in living up to God's ideals at times. At that juncture, the second function of the law activates and points its finger at us, declaring that we are sinners and therefore subject to eternal death (Romans 6:23). "By the law is the knowledge of sin" (Romans 3:20).

But the law doesn't stop there. It moves on in its third function to lead sinners to Jesus for forgiveness and salvation (Galatians 3:24). When we come to Him on our knees and confess our sins, the Bible tells us that God will "forgive us our sins" and "cleanse us from all unrighteousness" (1 John 1:9). Thus the law leads us to the gospel. And in the word *gospel*, we find the true meaning and function of the law.

9

Christians and God's Law

*So then, the Law itself is holy, and
the commandment is holy, right, and good.*
—Romans 7:12, GNT

Recently, a man told me that he was free from the law, that God had done away with the law for Christians, and that he had been liberated from the law because he was under the new covenant.

To say the least, his sincere assertions caught me by surprise, because the Bible teaches just the opposite. Hebrews 8 tells us that God will not only forgive the sins of new-covenant Christians (verse 12) but that He will put His laws "in their mind and write them on their hearts" (verse 10).

Thus according to the Bible, the new-covenant experience is just the opposite of being free from the law. To the contrary, new-covenant believers will have it engraved in their hearts and minds. Keeping such a law will be at the core of their daily experience.

Was the law done away with?

Some Bible students claim that the law was done away with at the cross. Apparently, they have never paid much attention to Jesus, who tells us: "Do not think that I came to destroy the Law or the Prophets. I did not come to destroy but to fulfill [fill up the meaning]. For assuredly, I say to you, till heaven and earth pass away, one jot or one tittle will by no means pass from the law till all is fulfilled. Whoever therefore breaks one of the least of these commandments, and teaches men so, shall be called least in the kingdom of heaven; but whoever does and teaches them, he shall be called great in the kingdom of heaven" (Matthew 5:17–19).

Then to leave people with no excuse about the Ten Commandments being important in Christian living, Jesus went on to explain or complete the meaning of several of the commandments, including those on murder (verses 21, 22) and adultery (verses 27–30). Apparently, somebody forgot to tell Jesus about a lawless new covenant.

They must have neglected to tell Paul also. In his great book on salvation by grace through faith, he asks a crucial question: "Do we then make void the law through faith?" Going on to answer his own question, he exclaims, "Certainly not! On the contrary, we establish the law" (Romans 3:31). I should point out that to establish something means just the opposite of doing away with it.

Christians and God's Law

Later in the book of Romans, Paul declares that "the law is holy, and the commandment holy and just and good" (Romans 7:12). And if that isn't enough, he goes on to point out that "the law is spiritual" (verse 14) and repeats his comment on the goodness of the law (verse 16). With all those good things to say about the law, Paul would probably wonder why anyone would want to do away with it.

James is also one who had good things to say about the law, calling it "the perfect law of liberty" (James 1:25). Here he touches on an important point. After all, it is those who keep the law who are free. That is true in the spiritual world just as it is in the civic, where those who disobey the law are behind bars. In the spiritual realm, they stand condemned by the broken law (Romans 3:20). Grace, in fact, is only necessary because of the condemning function of the law. If there were no law, there would be no sin, and if there were no sin, there would be no need for grace. Thus those who are so anxious to do away with law actually do away with grace at the same time.

But wasn't the law nailed to the cross?

Some may ask, Wasn't the law done away with because it was nailed to the cross? Good question. Probably the favorite verse on that issue is Colossians 2:14, which some believe teaches that the law was nailed to the cross. But what does the passage really teach? Verse

13 speaks of those who had been dead in and condemned by their sins but who had been forgiven those sins. Then verse 14 notes that God has "wiped out the handwriting of requirements that was against us, which was contrary to us. And He has taken it out of the way, having nailed it to the cross."

What in those verses, we need to ask, was nailed to the cross? In order to answer that question, we need to discover the identity of "the handwriting of requirements that was against us" and that "was contrary to us."

Verse 13 indicates that the issue being discussed is the penalty of sin, which leads to death but was forgiven. That context helps us understand what was nailed to the cross. But we also need to ask about "the handwriting of requirements that was against us" and "contrary to us." Here we need to join Paul who taught that while the law was good and spiritual, the broken law condemns sinners. It is not the good law of liberty that is against us but the penalty of the broken law. The requirement of the law is that "the wages of sin is death" (Romans 6:23). The only way out of that penal requirement, which is certainly contrary to us, is to accept Jesus as our Savior who died on the cross to set us free from the penalty of sin. Thus it was that penalty that was nailed to the cross. That conclusion lines up with the context of Colossians 2:14 and the theology found in the rest of the New Testament.

The importance of new-covenant law

Jesus emphasized the importance of the law for new-covenant Christians when He told His disciples, "If you love Me, keep My commandments" (John 14:15). That seems to be clear enough. But some must have missed the point. So in his first letter, John makes it so clear that no one can miss the postcross teaching of the New Testament on the topic: "He who says, 'I know Him,' and does not keep His commandments, is a liar, and the truth is not in him" (1 John 2:4). And in case that is not enough, the book of Revelation goes out of its way to tell us that at the end of time God will have a people who keep His commandments (Revelation 12:17; 14:12). At that time in history, those who are against God's law are pictured as linking up with the devil to fight against those who keep God's commandments.

The issue is clear enough in the Bible. The only question for us is which side we will be on in that last great conflict.

10

A Weekly Gift From Jesus

"Observe the Sabbath and keep it holy. You have six days in which to do your work, but the seventh day is a day of rest dedicated to me. On that day no one is to work— neither you, your children, your slaves, your animals, nor the foreigners who live in your country. In six days I, the LORD, made the earth, the sky, the seas, and everything in them, but on the seventh day I rested. That is why I, the LORD, blessed the Sabbath and made it holy."
—Exodus 20:8–11, GNT

"The Sabbath is for the Jews."

Really? How can that possibly be true when God gave the Sabbath two thousand years before there were any Jews? Those questions take us to the surprising topic of Jesus and the Sabbath.

Jesus and the Sabbath

Jesus claims that "the Sabbath was made for man, and not man for the Sabbath. Therefore the Son of Man is also Lord of the Sabbath" (Mark 2:27, 28). There are several important points in those verses. The first is that the Sabbath was made for "man" or all people rather than for the Jews. That thought is based upon the fact that the seventh-day Sabbath was first given to humanity at the end of Creation week. Genesis 2 tells us that "on the seventh day God ended His work . . . , and He rested on the seventh day from all His work. . . . Then God blessed the seventh day and sanctified it, because in it He rested from all His work" (verses 2, 3). Thus the Bible is clear that Jesus knew what He was talking about when He said that the Sabbath was made for "man" or all humanity rather than for the Jews.

But what, you may be thinking, *did Jesus mean when He claimed to be Lord of the Sabbath?* That is an especially important question since it disagrees with many who believe that the "Lord's Day" (Revelation 1:10) is Sunday rather than the seventh day of the week. Jesus put all such ideas to rest when He proclaimed Himself to be "Lord of the Sabbath" (Mark 2:28).

But how can that be? Go back to Genesis 1:26, 27, in which the Bible teaches in the words "Let Us" that all the Members of the divine Trinity participated in the creation of this world. That thought agrees with the New Testament's teaching that Jesus participated in Creation. We read in John 1:1, 3 that "in the beginning was the Word [Jesus], . . . and the Word was God. . . . All things were made through Him, and without Him nothing was made" (see also Hebrews

1:2; Colossians 1:16). With that plain teaching in mind, it is easy to see what Jesus meant when He claimed that He was "Lord of the Sabbath." Thus the Bible teaches that the "Lord's Day" is the seventh-day Sabbath—Jesus' weekly gift to His followers.

Sabbath as a sign of Creation and Redemption

Jesus not only gave the seventh-day Sabbath at Creation, but He also was instrumental in setting forth the Sabbath in the Ten Commandments. After all, Jesus plainly taught that He was the "I AM" who met Moses at the burning bush (Exodus 3:14; John 8:58). And He was the "I am" who gave the Ten Commandments to Moses (Exodus 20:2).

Thus we find that Jesus not only provided the Sabbath for all humanity at Creation but that He re-emphasized the seventh-day Sabbath at Sinai. In fact, the Sabbath commandment explicitly teaches that the weekly Sabbath is to be a reminder that God created the earth in seven days (Exodus 20:8–11).

But here we have an interesting teaching. Because when Moses, under divine inspiration, summarized the Ten Commandments at the end of his earthly life, he related the Sabbath commandment to God's redeeming act in saving His people from Egyptian bondage (Deuteronomy 5:12–15). As a result, the Sabbath flashes forth two great messages to worshipers every week; namely, that Jesus is not only the Creator but also the Redeemer who saves His people from the bondage of sin.

The change of the Sabbath
One of the plainest teachings of the New Testament is that not only did Jesus Himself keep the Sabbath (Luke 4:16) but that His apostles and their followers worshiped on that day after He rose from the grave (Acts 13:14, 44; 16:13; 17:1, 2; 18:4).

Since that is true, we are forced to ask why the day of worship for most Christians is now Sunday rather than the Sabbath of Jesus and His New Testament followers. Part of the answer is a misunderstanding of such passages as John 20:1; Acts 20:7; and 1 Corinthians 16:2—these verses mention the first day of the week but provide absolutely no authority for changing God's day of worship. The most interesting of those verses is John 20:1 and its parallel passages in the other Gospels. Many people take those passages as a justification that Christians are to keep the first day of the week as a memorial of Christ's resurrection. That teaching has three problems. First, the passages provide no justification for a change. Second, it contradicts the teachings of Jesus and His apostles. Third, the New Testament is clear that it is baptism rather than Sunday that is the memorial of Christ's resurrection (Romans 6:3, 4).

While the misunderstanding of certain Bible texts

is related to the "change" of the Sabbath, even more to the point is Daniel 7:25, which plainly teaches that a power would arise that would attempt to change God's law, especially as it related to time. With that prophecy in mind, it is of interest that the only entity that historically has claimed the authority to change the Sabbath has been the Roman Catholic Church. Thus the *Convert's Catechism of Catholic Doctrine*, after noting that the biblical Sabbath is Saturday, goes on to claim that "we observe Sunday instead of Saturday because the Catholic Church transferred the solemnity from Saturday to Sunday."[1] Interestingly, the Protestant Reformers followed the Catholic Church on that teaching.

The Sabbath in the twenty-first century

One of the neglected teachings of the New Testament is the fact that the true Sabbath will be restored before Christ returns. Revelation 12:17 and 14:12 explicitly teach that God will have a commandment-keeping people at the end of time. And between those two verses, Revelation 14:7 emphasizes the fact that at the end of time God's followers will "worship Him who made heaven and earth, the sea and springs of water." That passage is a specific reference to Christ's Sabbath rest in Genesis 2:2, 3 and Exodus 20:8–11. As a result, the keeping of God's seventh-day Sabbath is just as important today as it has been all down through history.

The good news is that Jesus is still Lord of the Sabbath and that He wants us to meet with Him weekly on that day to celebrate Him as Creator and Redeemer.

---

1. Peter Geiermann, *The Convert's Catechism of Catholic Doctrine* (St. Louis, MO: Herder, 1946), 50.

11

Time for Life's Most Important Things

"The Sabbath was made for the good of human beings; they were not made for the Sabbath."
—Mark 2:27, GNT

Modern people are always in a hurry. Business drives our days, whereas family, time for Bible study and prayer, and even God get pushed to the corners of our lives. Some of us are frustrated by the constant push of daily events, while others of us don't even have time to care.

God knew that sinful humans would mess up time just as they have every other aspect of their lives. As a result, He has provided us with a weekly "time-out" so that we can slow down and get perspective on the meaning of life and build a healthier life. He called that time-out "Sabbath."

Messing up the Sabbath
Human beings have the ability to confuse everything.

The Jews of Christ's day had done so with Jesus' gift of the Sabbath. Their whole approach to the topic transformed the day of weekly blessing into a disaster area.

For some of them, the problem was that they hoped to gain salvation through Sabbath keeping. The apostle Paul put an end to that line of thinking when he wrote that no one could be justified by keeping the law (Romans 3:20). More subtle was the temptation to view the Sabbath in negative terms. The Jews of Christ's day had specified thirty-nine categories of work forbidden on the Sabbath. Beyond that, they had developed more than fifteen hundred rules related to the Sabbath.

By the time of Jesus, the keeping of the Sabbath had become a burden—a list of dos and don'ts with the don'ts predominating. The Jews viewed the day of rest as if God first had a Sabbath and then had created people to keep it. In effect, God had a group of Sabbath slaves, and He was watching to make sure they kept all the rules.

Jesus revolutionizes the Sabbath

Jesus, the Creator of the Sabbath, turned the thinking of the Jews upside down. His was a positive view. To Him people were not made because God had a law that needed to be kept, but rather "the Sabbath was made for man [people]" (Mark 2:27). That is, people had needs, and God in His love provided them with a Sabbath in order to fulfill those needs. The Sabbath was given to make the lives of men and women better in every aspect—physically, mentally, socially, and spiritually.

The context of Jesus' teaching regarding the Sabbath in Mark 2:27, 28 illustrates Jesus' positive view of the Sabbath. Mark 2:23–26 and 3:1–6 illustrate the meaning of the Sabbath being made for people rather than people for the Sabbath by demonstrating that the day was given as a time to fill human needs in terms of healing and the necessities of life. In fact, the Sabbath is best viewed as a gift of grace to make life better and a gift to meet human need.

Those needs come in several flavors. Most basic is the need for physical rest. God knew that some of us would be workaholics, who would be tempted to go full speed seven days a week, while others of us would be tempted to work seven days a week just to meet necessary expenses. But He also knew that such a lifestyle would come with a physical price because the human body was not made to work incessantly. We need rest. As a result, He provided us with the Sabbath as a time of physical restoration. The past twenty years has seen a flurry of religious and even secular books on the wisdom of one day of rest in seven.

But here we have a challenge. Physical rest implies more than sleep. Any animal can rest in sleep. But human rest is above that of animals. It means rest from the usual round of gainful work so that we might have time to grow to be more like God in every way.

As a result, the Sabbath as a gift of God's grace provides time for people to fulfill their spiritual needs through Bible study, worship, and refreshing our souls in nature. Beyond that, the Sabbath gives us time to fill our social needs by worshiping together in church, by spending quality time with our families, by fellowshiping with our friends, and by helping others understand God's Word. All in all, the Sabbath, from Christ's perspective, is the very best day of the week. It is a gift of grace for healing and health.

Making space for the blessing

But in a less-than-perfect world, even positive blessings have negative implications. Another way of making my point is to say that you can't add to human activity without subtracting something.

That insight is exactly where the Ten Commandments picks up the topic. "Remember the Sabbath day, to keep it holy," we read in Exodus 20. "Six days you shall labor and do all your work, but the seventh day is the Sabbath of the LORD your God. In it you shall do no work: you, nor your son, nor your daughter, nor your . . . servant. . . . For in six days the LORD made the heavens and the earth, . . . and rested the seventh day. Therefore the LORD blessed the Sabbath day and hallowed it" (verses 8–11).

There are several things that we should notice about

the Sabbath commandment. The first is that we are to cease all gainful employment on that day. That makes sense. After all, if I am to have time to let God make the Sabbath a blessing in my life, He will have to free up some time. But here we need to note how specific the command is. It does not say *a* seventh day (like resting every Wednesday) but *the* seventh day (Saturday). The command does not give any options here for two reasons: One, it allows all His people to have time to worship together. A second is that it honors God as Creator.

A second thing to notice about the commandment is that it tells us not to hire other people to work for us on that day. That aspect of the Sabbath is why I do not do my shopping or hire people to fix my food in a restaurant on the Sabbath. It is a day totally given over to God, my family, other people, and spiritual activities.

A third thing to note about the command is that of following the example of both God the Father and Jesus (Genesis 2:2, 3; Luke 4:16).

A fourth thing is that God blessed the Sabbath and set it aside for holy use.

A final thing to note is that God commands us to "remember the Sabbath." It is of interest that this is the only one of the Ten Commandments that begins with "remember." Perhaps that is because you and I are tempted to forget or neglect God's holy day.

12

A Public Testimony of Our Faith

> *Then Peter said to them, "Repent, and let every one of you be baptized in the name of Jesus Christ for the remission of sins; and you shall receive the gift of the Holy Spirit."*
> —Acts 2:38

Some sprinkle, some pour, some dunk (immerse).

While churches may differ on the way to baptize, we need to discover what the Bible teaches on the topic of both the method and the meaning of this important aspect of Christianity. In the process, we will discover that the method and the meaning of baptism are closely related. On the other hand, when method and meaning are disconnected, they each become distorted.

Even though churches differ over the method and meaning of baptism, all agree on its importance. After all, some of the last words of Jesus were that His disciples were to go into all the world, "baptizing" in the name of the Trinity and "teaching them . . . to observe all things that I have commanded" (Matthew 28:19, 20).

The biblical method of baptism

The New Testament teaching on baptism begins with John the Baptist. A hint as to the method he used is found in John 3:23, in which we find him baptizing at one location because there was "much water." In other words, baptism was not something that could be done with a cup or other small measure of water. We discover that to be the case in the baptism of Jesus, in which we find Him coming up out of the water after being baptized by John (Matthew 3:16). Similarly, when Philip baptized the Ethiopian in Acts 8, they went "down into the water" before the baptism, and they "came up out of the water" afterward (verses 38, 39).

The biblical picture is consistently one of baptism by immersion (being completely covered in water) and no other. That understanding is consistent with the very meaning of the Greek word *baptizō* (to baptize), which literally means "to put or go under water"[1] or "to immerge, submerge."[2] It is the word used when a piece of cloth is submerged in dye. Baptism is never viewed as sprinkling or pouring in the New Testament.

The biblical meaning of baptism

The clearest teaching regarding the meaning of baptism in the New Testament is found in Romans 6:3, 4, in which Paul compares baptism to the burial and resurrection of Jesus: "Do you not know that as many of us as were baptized into Christ Jesus were baptized

A Public Testimony of Our Faith

into His death? Therefore we were buried with Him through baptism into death, that just as Christ was raised from the dead by the glory of the Father, even so we also should walk in newness of life." Here we find the meaning of baptism being likened to a watery burial and a resurrection from that watery grave (cf. Colossians 2:12, 13). Thus we find that the meaning of baptism harmonizes perfectly with the method of baptism described above and the dictionary meaning of the Greek word for *baptism*. Once again, no model of baptism fits the biblical teaching except baptism by immersion.

Another important aspect of the meaning of baptism as it relates to New Testament Christianity is the relationship of baptism to understanding. Jesus touches on that topic in Matthew 28:19, 20 when He relates baptism to teaching. And Peter expands on the relationship when he urges his hearers to "repent, and let every one of you be baptized in the name of Jesus Christ" (Acts 2:38). Since repentance indicates not only knowledge of what is to be repented of but also faith in Christ, it is obvious that belief is a precondition to baptism. We find the same picture in Acts 16:30–33, in which the Philippian jailer asked Paul what he needed to do in order to be saved. The apostle's answer was that he needed to believe (verse 31). That statement was followed by instruction in "the word of the Lord" (verse 32) and baptism (verse 33). The New

Testament pattern is clear and consistent. First comes instruction and belief in the teachings of the Bible, then comes baptism. People in the New Testament always understood the teachings of the Bible before they were baptized.

The connection between instruction, understanding, repentance, and baptism contradicts the widespread practice of infant baptism. The Bible knows nothing of infant baptism, which reverses the New Testament order. Whereas infant baptism implies baptism before knowledge and repentance, the Bible is clear that instruction, understanding, and repentance must take place before baptism. Thus it is that many people think they have had a biblical baptism as infants; but from the perspective of the New Testament, they are truly unbaptized.

Baptism and the church

People sometimes want to be baptized without joining the church. That is not the New Testament teaching. Paul makes that clear when he writes that Christians are "all baptized into one body" (1 Corinthians 12:13).

Here we have come to another important Bible teaching. The New Testament knows nothing of solitary Christians who stand alone in the world. The New Testament is consistent in all its pictures of the church: becoming a Christian means not only being baptized but becoming a part of the body of Christ, which has many members with Jesus as the head (Ephesians 1:22, 23; 2:19–22). Thus biblical baptism is the ceremony by which a person joins the church or body of Christ.

Baptism by water and Spirit

Jesus made it clear that no one could enter His kingdom except by being born by water (baptism) and the Holy Spirit (John 3:3, 5). Here we find an interesting combination that some people would like to separate. But we do so only at our spiritual peril because Jesus is teaching that water baptism is not enough. Nothing magic happens at baptism. To the contrary, baptism is only an outward and public experience that signifies that the new Christian has truly been convicted of sin and righteousness by the Holy Spirit (John 16:8) and has experienced a new spiritual birth (John 3:5). Thus baptism is an outward sign of an inward experience in each believer. Needless to say, Christ's desire for each of us is that we might be baptized by both the water and the Spirit and become members of His eternal church.

---

1. William D. Mounce, ed., *Mounce's Complete Expository Dictionary of Old and New Testament Words* (Grand Rapids, MI: Zondervan, 2006), 52.

2. Joseph Thayer, trans. and ed., *A Greek-English Lexicon of the New Testament*, corrected ed. (New York: American Book Co., 1889), 94.

13

What Happens When We Die?

We do not want you to be uninformed, brethren, about those who are asleep, so that you will not grieve as do the rest who have no hope. For if we believe that Jesus died and rose again, even so God will bring with Him those who have fallen asleep in Jesus.
—1 Thessalonians 4:13, 14, NASB

The law of the tombstone is universal—everybody gets one. There are some things that are uncertain in life. But of one thing we can be sure: every one of us will die. That certainly has led men and women everywhere to wonder what happens at death.

The Bible on life and death

The best answer to our questions about death is found in the Bible. But before we look at its teaching on death, it is important to examine the nature of life.

The clearest passage on the topic is Genesis 2:7, "And the LORD God formed man of the dust of the ground, and breathed into his nostrils the breath of life; and man became a living being."

What Happens When We Die?

The basic formula is simple enough:

dust + breath = living being

The dust, of course, is the physical material that makes up our bodies. The breath is the life-giving power of God that energizes the physical material. Here we find an important point; namely, that *breath* in the biblical languages also means "spirit." Therefore when God infuses the dust with His spirit, a living being is created. That term *living being* is also an interesting one since it can also be translated as "soul." With that understanding, we can return to the Creation formula utilizing words that people often use when speaking about death.

dust + spirit = soul

Those are important words, since many people believe that the spirit, or soul, returns to God at death. However, we need to ask what the Bible teaches on the topic.

Here the Bible is crystal clear. A helpful passage is Ecclesiastes 12:7. It represents death as the exact opposite of life. "Then," we read, "the dust will return to the earth as it was, and the spirit [breath] will return to God who gave it." Once again the formula is plain:

dust - spirit = death

What, then, takes place at death? The Creation process is reversed. The dust, or bodily matter, goes into the grave, and the energizing spirit, or breath of life, returns to God. Here is an important point. The word *spirit* is used hundreds of times in the Bible. But it is never used as an intelligent entity capable of existence apart from a physical body. That which returns to God is simply the life principle imparted by God in the creation of life.

That is understandable. But what happens to the soul? The Bible is clear on that point, teaching that the soul or person ceases to exist.

But aren't all people created with immortal souls? Not according to the Bible, which plainly teaches that only God is immortal (1 Timothy 6:15, 16). On the other hand, the Scriptures also teach that those who have followed Jesus will receive the gift of immortality when He returns at the end of earthly history (1 Corinthians 15:53). But no humans have immortality until that time.

Then where did the teaching of the immortal soul come from? Its origin is not the Bible. Rather, it came into the church through Greek philosophy, especially through the influence of Plato. It is a teaching diametrically opposed to the clear word of God in the Bible.

Death as unconscious sleep

The Bible is consistent on the topic of death. The body, or dust, goes into the grave, while the spirit, or breath of life, returns to God who gave it.

This teaching harmonizes with Jesus' teaching that death is like a deep sleep. His clearest passage on the topic is in relation to His friend Lazarus. In John 11, He tells His disciples that "Lazarus sleeps" (verse 11). But they misunderstand, interpreting Jesus' remark as "taking rest in sleep" (verse 13). As a result, "Jesus said to them plainly, 'Lazarus is dead' " (verse 14). In that passage, Jesus could not have been clearer that death is like a deep sleep (see also Daniel 12:2; 1 Thessalonians 4:13, 14; Acts 7:60).

The Bible's teaching on death as a sleep agrees with its description of those who are in their graves. It represents the dead as having no memory (Psalm 6:5) or praise for God (Psalm 115:17). Psalm 146:4 is one of the clearest on death and its unconscious nature: "His spirit [breath] departs, he [the dust] returns to his earth [the grave]; in that very day his plans perish."

Beyond death is resurrection

The Bible is consistent in both testaments in presenting death as an unconscious deep sleep. But it is not an endless sleep. To the contrary, both testaments present resurrection as an awakening from the sleep of death as God once again infuses the breath of life into the bodily dust and men and women are raised to life.

Paul makes that teaching crystal clear, telling the believers in Thessalonica that he does not want them "to be ignorant" about those "who have fallen asleep. . . . For the Lord Himself will descend from heaven with a shout, with the voice of an archangel, and with the trumpet of God. And the dead in Christ will rise first. Then we who are alive . . . shall be caught up together with them in the clouds to meet the Lord in the air. And thus shall we always be with the Lord" (1 Thessalonians 4:13, 16, 17; cf. Daniel 12:2; John 5:28, 29).

It is at that resurrection, or awakening from the sleep of death, that those who have accepted Jesus will "put on immortality" (1 Corinthians 15:53), which means that they will no longer be subject to the possibility of death. Thus Paul can proclaim that "death is swallowed up in victory" (verse 54) at the resurrection that takes place at the second coming of Jesus.

Choosing life in Christ

The good news for Christians is that death is not the end. The Bible presents it as a deep sleep from which they will be awakened when Jesus returns. That is why believers in Jesus have no fear of death.

This teaching is important for you and me. We need

to choose today to follow the Lord of life so that we might be with that group that rises to meet Him in the air when He comes again to put an end to death forever for those who have chosen to walk with Him.

14

What Is Jesus Doing Now?

We have such a High Priest, who sits at the right of the throne of the Divine Majesty in heaven. He serves as high priest in the Most Holy Place, that is, in the real tent which was put up by the Lord, not by human hands.
—Hebrews 8:1, 2, GNT

Have you ever wondered what happened to Jesus? After all, we know that He ascended to heaven and that He repeatedly told His disciples that He would return again in the clouds of heaven to take His followers to their eternal reward (Matthew 24; Acts 1:11; 1 Thessalonians 4:13–18). But that was two thousand years ago. What has He been doing for all that time?

That is an excellent question. The good news is that the Bible is not silent on the subject. In fact, one of the twenty-seven books of the New Testament is entirely devoted to the topic, while most of the others shed light upon it. The book of Hebrews tells us that Jesus has been representing His followers as their "High Priest," as "a Minister of the sanctuary and of the true tabernacle which the Lord erected, and not man" (Hebrews 8:1, 2).

What Is Jesus Doing Now?

Here we have a topic extensively treated in the Bible—but one on which many churches are largely silent. But the clear teaching of Scripture is that Jesus has been ministering for us in the heavenly sanctuary ever since His return to heaven.

That is clear enough, you may be thinking. *But what does His heavenly ministry mean? What is He doing there?*

The earthly model

To answer those questions, we need to briefly examine the earthly sanctuary and its priestly ministry. After all, Hebrews 8:5 indicates that the earthly sanctuary ministry was an illustration of Jesus' heavenly work (cf. Hebrews 9:9; 10:1).

That thought takes us back to Exodus 25:8, 9, in which Moses was commanded by God to build a sanctuary, or tabernacle, after the "pattern" of the one in heaven (see also Exodus 25:40; Hebrews 8:5). The earthly sanctuary was divided into two sections, described as the Holy Place and the Most Holy Place.

Ministry in the first of those apartments took place on a daily basis as the priests sacrificed lambs and made other offerings in the courtyard of the sanctuary and applied the blood of the sacrifices in the Holy Place. Part of that daily routine included the priestly mediation of forgiveness for God's people.

The ministry in the Most Holy Place, or the second apartment, took place once a year on the Day of

Atonement, which represented a day of judgment and cleansing of God's people at the end of the Jewish religious year (see Leviticus 16).

Jesus' ministry in the heavenly sanctuary

The important thing to remember about the earthly sanctuary is that it represented a model of the plan of salvation that would be carried out by Jesus, the true High Priest. Thus it is that the daily animal sacrifices represented the death of Jesus, the ultimate "Lamb of God who takes away the sin of the world" (John 1:29). And just as the foundation of the earthly sanctuary service was the offering of the sacrificial lamb, so it was that Jesus died "once" for all people in order "to put away sin by the sacrifice of Himself" (Hebrews 9:26). Here is the heart of the gospel: "Christ died for our sins" (1 Corinthians 15:3). After that death, He "rose again" (verse 4) and ascended "into heaven" (Acts 1:11) where He became our "High Priest" in the heavenly sanctuary (Hebrews 8:1).

But exactly what is Jesus doing as our High Priest? This is where the earthly sanctuary model becomes important because it was provided to illustrate the ministry of Christ. Just as the sacrificial lambs represented Jesus the Lamb of God, so the earthly priesthood represented Jesus the true High Priest and the earthly sanctuary represented the true one in heaven. As a result, we can learn a lot about Jesus' heavenly work through a study of the earthly model.

And just as that model represented the priesthood as having two phases, depicted by the ministries in the two apartments, so it is that Jesus' ministry also has two phases. The first of those phases is the ministry of mediation or intercession. On a continual basis as God's people come to Him in prayer, Jesus provides forgiveness based on their faith in His death on the cross. Thus Hebrews 7:25 tells us that He is "able to save to the uttermost those who come to God through Him, since He always lives to make intercession for them" (cf. Romans 8:34). First John is especially helpful in our understanding when it proclaims that "if we confess our sins, He is faithful and just to forgive us our sins" (1 John 1:9). John ties that ministry of forgiveness to Jesus' sanctuary ministry in the next few verses. "If anyone sins, we have an Advocate with the Father, Jesus Christ the righteous" who died for the sins of "the whole world" (1 John 2:1, 2).

The real good news about Jesus in His ministry of intercession and forgiveness is that He, having become human in the Incarnation, understands our weaknesses. As a result, we can "come boldly to the throne of grace" to "obtain mercy and find grace to help in time of need" (Hebrews 4:15, 16).

Before moving away from the daily ministry of Christ, there is one point on which some people have become confused. The Bible plainly teaches that there is "*one Mediator* between God and men, the Man Christ Jesus" (1 Timothy 2:5; emphasis added). In the New Testament era, there is no need for any other intercessors through an earthly priesthood or saints just as there is no need to make offerings or sacrifices of atonement. Jesus is the only Priest and Intercessor, and He died on the cross once for all people. Anything more than that is contrary to the New Testament's clear teachings and is therefore wrong and an insult to Christ.

The second phase of Christ's ministry in the Most Holy Place is a ministry of judgment at the end of time, just as the Jewish religious year ended in judgment on the Day of Atonement. We will have more to say on that topic in a future chapter.

What does this mean for me?

The teaching of the heavenly sanctuary is one of the most precious in the New Testament. It is in light of Christ's ministry in it that we come to Him in prayer day by day and have confidence not only for the forgiveness of our sins but also of vindication in the final judgment.

15

Jesus Hasn't Left Us in the Dark

*"Afterward I will pour out my Spirit on everyone:
your sons and daughters will proclaim my message;
your old people will have dreams,
and your young people will see visions."*
—Joel 2:28, GNT

Some years ago I read a book claiming that all modern prophets were false and that any religious group that had a modern prophet was a cult and should be avoided. The book went on to notify the readers that the gift of prophecy had ceased with the death of the last apostle.

I had no doubt about the author's convictions on the topic, but I wondered if the Bible taught the same thing. The first text I came across was Matthew 24:24, in which Jesus claims that in the last days "false prophets" would "rise and show great signs and wonders to deceive, if possible, even the elect [God's people]."

Next, I read 1 Corinthians 13:8–10, which definitely predicts an end to the prophetic gift. But as I examined those verses, I noted that this ending would not come until the second advent of Jesus, when the "perfect has come" (verse 10).

Spiritual gifts will guide the church

This conclusion definitely agreed with Ephesians 4:11–13, in which Paul lists the gift of prophecy along with several other enabling gifts of the Holy Spirit and notes that they were given by God for "the equipping of the saints for the work of ministry, for the edifying of the body of Christ, till we all come to the unity of the faith and of the knowledge of the Son of God."

That statement helped me see that spiritual gifts, including that of prophets, would be in the church until Christ returned. After all, the saints still need to be equipped for ministry; the body, or church, of Christ still needs to be built up; and God's people still need to be united in faith and the knowledge of God's Son.

Ephesians 4 was clear enough on the topic, but the passage that helped me see most plainly that the gift of prophecy would guide the church until the end of time was Joel 2:28–31. In that passage, God tells His people that in the future He would "pour out" His "Spirit on all flesh; your sons and your daughters shall prophecy, your old men shall dream dreams, your young men shall see visions" (verse 28). While Peter claimed a partial fulfillment of that promise in Acts 2:16–21, the ultimate fulfillment, according to Joel 2:30, 31 will not take place until the signs of Christ's second coming are seen in the heavens at "the coming of the great and awesome day of the Lord" (verse 31). (On the heavenly signs of Christ's coming, see Matthew 24:29, 30; Mark 13:24–26; Luke 21:11, 25–27; Revelation 6:12, 13.)

As I read Ephesians 4 and Joel 2, I realized that God had plainly revealed to the biblical prophets in both the Old and New Testaments that He would provide the prophetic gift to guide His people on Earth until the Second Coming. *But*, I thought to myself, *there are some really weird people who have claimed to have prophecies from God. How can I keep from being misled?*

The command to test the prophets

That question led me to 1 Thessalonians 5:19–21: "Do not quench the Spirit. Do not despise prophecies. Test all things; hold fast what is good." Here is a passage of utmost importance for God's people. Apparently, some church members in Paul's day were downplaying the importance of spiritual gifts (verse 19) and were especially against those who claimed that they had the gift of prophecy (verse 20). That situation led the apostle to counsel against both an automatic rejection of those claiming the prophetic gift and an automatic acceptance of their claims. In place of such mindless, emotional reactions, Paul counseled the Thessalonians (and us) to examine such claims by testing them and cherishing that which is good (verse 21).

While 1 Thessalonians 5:19–21 is helpful in its cautious counsel on the prophetic gift, the passage does not provide us with any specific ideas on how to test for the genuineness of those who claim to have the gift. The good news is that other parts of the Bible do. Thus we find Jesus warning that His followers needed to "beware of false prophets, who come to you in sheep's clothing, but inwardly they are ravenous wolves" (Matthew 7:15). The only safety in the face of such claims, He asserted, is to test them "by their fruits" (verses 16, 20). The implications of that counsel are that true prophets will live godly lives and the results of following their counsel will lead to a good life.

A second biblical test is that the teaching of a true prophet will not contradict the teachings of the Bible. Thus Isaiah writes, "To the law and to the testimony! If they do not speak according to this word, it is because there is no light in them" (Isaiah 8:20). This is a very important point because there are many in our day who claim to have the prophetic gift or some other gift from the Holy Spirit (such as tongues), and these people teach things that contradict the instruction God has given His people in the Bible. All such, according to the tests set forth in Scripture, are false prophets.

A third test is found in 1 John 4: "Beloved, do not believe every spirit, but test the spirits, whether they are of God; because many false prophets have gone out into the world. By this you know the Spirit of

God: Every spirit that confesses that Jesus Christ has come in the flesh is of God, and every spirit that does not confess that Jesus Christ has come in the flesh is not of God" (verses 1–3). In short, a true prophet will acknowledge Christ's humanity as well as His deity. Beyond that, it goes without saying, a true prophet will be clear on God's free forgiveness through Christ's death and resurrection (1 Corinthians 15:1–4, 12–20; Galatians 1:9; Ephesians 2:8–10).

Probably the most basic test is that a true prophet will point people to Jesus and the word of God in the Bible. All too many so-called prophets point people to themselves and to their own prophecies. That is a sure sign that they are pointing and leading in the wrong direction.

God still speaks
The best news about 1 Thessalonians 5:19–21 and other passages on the gifts of the Spirit is that God has not left us in the dark. He can still speak to His people through the gift of prophecy in the twenty-first century. Joel 2, in fact, tells us that those of God's people who live near the end of Earth's history can expect to see a revival of the true gift of prophecy.

16

God's Last Message to a Dying World

Then I saw another angel flying high in the air, with an eternal message of Good News to announce to the peoples of the earth, to every race, tribe, language, and nation. He said in a loud voice, "Honor God and praise his greatness! For the time has come for him to judge all people. Worship him who made heaven, earth, sea, and the springs of water!"
—Revelation 14:6, 7, GNT

One of the best-kept secrets in the entire Bible is found in Revelation 14:6–12. Of course, God never desired it to be a secret. To the contrary, He wanted it shouted from the housetops and proclaimed with a "loud voice" throughout the world (verse 7). But for some unexplainable reason, that passage has been almost totally ignored by most churches.

Before we look at those special verses, we need to emphasize the fact that the book of Revelation in its first verse tells us that it is a book from and about Jesus Christ. It is a book from our Lord and Savior, telling us what will take place throughout Christian history and especially those events that will be important near Earth's end.

The place of Revelation 14:6–12 in history and the message of the first angel

The end of human history is what Revelation 14 is all about. Verse 14 begins a graphic picture of Jesus' second coming.

As a result, the proclamation of the three angels' messages found in verses 6–12 are Christ's final messages to the world immediately before the Second Advent. As such, they are of the greatest importance. They are the messages that the Lord of the church desires to be given to the world at the end of earthly history.

The first of those three messages is found in Revelation 14:6, 7, "Then I saw another angel flying in the midst of heaven, having the everlasting gospel to preach to those who dwell on the earth—to every nation, tribe, tongue, and people—saying with a loud voice, 'Fear God and give glory to Him, for the hour of His judgment has come; and worship Him who made heaven and earth, the sea and springs of water.' "

We should note several things about that message. First, it is a gospel message. And all Christians know what the gospel is—that Jesus died for our sins (1 Corinthians 15:1–3). But a dead Savior does nobody any good. Thus the gospel also includes His resurrection from the dead (verse 4), which is an event that guarantees the resurrection of His followers (Revelation 1:18; 1 Thessalonians 4:13–18; 1 Corinthians 15:51–55). That is truly good news, but it took place two thousand years ago and people are still dying. As a result, the book of Revelation emphasizes the certain fact that Jesus will come again to rescue His people and take them home. The everlasting gospel in the book of Revelation includes the Second Advent, which is the focal point of the book.

A second thing to note about the first angel's message is that it (along with the other two) will be proclaimed throughout the entire world. A third aspect of the first message is that it will announce the hour (time) of God's judgment. The Bible portrays social and religious conditions right before the Second Coming as being in a state of deterioration. In the face of that fact, part of Christ's last message for the world will be a warning of judgment to wake people up. Judgment, of course, has two edges. For those rebelling against God and His ways, it is a fearful thing (Revelation 6:15–17); but for God's people, it will be a time of rejoicing and vindication (Revelation 6:10; 18:20; Daniel 7:22).

A final characteristic of the first angel's message is that it uplifts God as the Creator. And here we have an important point—because the creatorship of God all through the Bible is tied to the honoring of God by keeping the seventh-day Sabbath as a remembrance of His creatorship. Thus we find in the Ten Commandments that His people are to "remember the Sabbath day" and "keep it holy" because God rested on the seventh day after creating for six (Exodus 20:8). That thought takes us back to Genesis 2:1–3, in which we discover the same truth centuries before any Jews existed. The plain fact is that the Sabbath was made at Creation for all humanity (Mark 2:27, 28) and not merely for the Jews. The first angel proclaims the fact that the seventh-day Sabbath will be preached to all the world right before the return of Christ. That fact is emphasized by its context, which twice tells us that God will have a people who keep all His commandments as the Second Advent approaches (Revelation 12:17; 14:12).

The second and third angels' messages

The second angel's message of Revelation 14:8 proclaims the fall of Babylon, which is a power pictured in both testaments as opposing God's will. Babylon first surfaces in Genesis 11:7, 8, in which it is tied to the confusion of tongues. By the end of history, it is still tied to confusion. But more serious than the confusion of tongues in seeking to overthrow God's will is misleading or confusing people on the authority of God's Word in relation to human authority—a confusion that will lead them to follow the commands of human beings rather than those of God.

The third angel's message contrasts those who will be worshiping the beast at the end of time (Revelation 14:9) with those who will be keeping the commandments of God (Revelation 14:12; cf. 12:17). Revelation 14:12 represents the climactic point in the chapter and is the absolutely final message Jesus commanded His church to give before He returns in verse 14. "Here," we read in verse 12, "is the patience of the saints; here are those who keep the commandments of God and the faith of Jesus."

Verse 12 has three parts. The first is its Advent orientation, which portrays a people who are patiently waiting for their Lord in spite of the long delay. The second aspect indicates what God's end-time people will be doing as they patiently await their Lord. They will be keeping the commandments of God (cf. Revelation 12:17). And here it is of interest to note that one of those commandments has already been included in verse 7—the seventh-day Sabbath that is a memorial of God's creative act. The third part of verse 12 is "the faith of Jesus," or "faith in Jesus" as many translations render the Greek. Thus God's final message is not only about waiting for the Second Advent and keeping all of God's commandments—but it also identifies the end-time faithful as having a personal, saving relationship with Jesus.

Such is the message that God commanded to be preached to the ends of the earth. After the preaching of the three angels' messages, Jesus comes in the clouds. As a result, we need to take Revelation 14:6–12 very seriously.

17

Judgment Is Good News

For sin pays its wage—death; but God's free gift is eternal life in union with Christ Jesus our Lord.
—Romans 6:23, GNT

Judgment! Here is a scary word. No one likes to be judged by other people but even less so by God, who knows even our thoughts. Some people consider this the most fearful teaching of the Bible.

The bad news: We are all under condemnation
Some people try to solve the problem of condemnation by denying that there will be a final judgment. But that won't work. The Bible is clear on the topic. Acts 17:31 tells us that God "has appointed a day on which He will judge the world." And Paul writes that "we must all appear before the judgment seat of Christ" for what we have done (2 Corinthians 5:10). And the apostle makes it clear in the first two chapters of Romans that no one "will escape the judgment of God" (Romans 2:3).

Judgment Is Good News

The Bible not only presents the fact of God's final judgment, but it also does a remarkably thorough job of describing that event. One of the most fascinating descriptions is found in Daniel 7. "I watched," said the prophet in reporting his vision, "till thrones were put in place. And the Ancient of Days was seated. . . . Ten thousand times ten thousand stood before Him. The court was seated, and the books were opened" (verses 9, 10).

That scene portrays the glorious throne room in God's temple in heaven, when multitudes of angels witness Earth's final judgment. Notice that the picture is one of judgment based on evidence in "books." God's judgment is not based on opinion or arbitrary whim but on solid evidence—evidence recorded in the "computer system" of the universe.

The Bible mentions the books of judgment several times. "Rejoice," said Jesus to the disciples, "because your names are written in heaven" (Luke 10:20). Paul wrote of his faithful fellow workers that their "names are in the Book of Life" (Philippians 4:3). And John the revelator pointed out that there were books other than the book of life from which people would be judged (Revelation 20:12).

So the existence of a record of every human life—whether it be a record of good or of evil, one that leads to exoneration or to condemnation—is well documented in the Bible. It is little wonder that fear of judgment has plagued the hearts of men and women.

The Bible even makes clear the legal standard of the final judgment—God's law (James 2:12). Over and over, the book of Romans calls our attention to the fact that the function of the law is to point out our sins (Romans 3:20; 4:15; 7:7).

So the function of the law is to hold up God's ideal before us and then to censure us when we fail to meet that ideal. When the law identifies us as sinners, it places us under condemnation as criminals in God's kingdom. And that is problematic because "all have sinned and fall short of the glory of God" (Romans 3:23). That is bad, but it gets worse since "the wages of sin is death" (Romans 6:23).

So where is the good news of judgment?

"Well," you may be asking by this time, "what can I do? How can I get this verdict changed?"

Some people seek to escape condemnation by being better, by keeping the law. But such individuals fail to understand that the law cannot save. It can point out our sin and tell us where we have gone wrong, but it was never given to be our savior.

And here is where the good news of judgment begins. The law points beyond our sin to Jesus and salvation through faith in His saving grace. It is because of Jesus that the judgment is good news. And that good news is based on the love of God.

Judgment Is Good News

Unlike modern judges, God is not neutral. He is actively on the side of those whom the devil is pointing an accusatory finger toward. One of the crucial facts of Scripture is that "God so loved the world [me] that He gave His only begotten Son, that whoever believes in Him should not perish but have everlasting life" (John 3:16). Or, as Paul put it, "God demonstrates His own love toward us, in that while we were still sinners, Christ died for us" (Romans 5:8).

That, my friend, is excellent news—the very best of good news. The wonder of wonders is that God is willing to credit Jesus' life and death to my name in the judgment if I am willing to accept Him by faith. That is why Paul could write that even though "the wages of sin is death, . . . the gift of God is eternal life in Christ Jesus our Lord" (Romans 6:23). And Jesus not only died for us, He is currently ministering for each of His followers as our "Advocate" in the heavenly sanctuary (1 John 2:1).

Because of Jesus, the judgment is always good news for those who follow Him. Or as the book of Daniel puts it, God's final judgment is "in favor of the saints" (Daniel 7:22).

Why judgment is a topic for rejoicing

Too many people have thought of the final judgment as a kind of medieval inquisition headed up by a vengeful God. Not so! God's purpose in the judgment is the vindication of believers through confirmation that they have accepted Jesus. It is God's aim to save as many people as possible so that He can take them home to heaven when Jesus returns a second time.

Those who accept Jesus by faith have nothing to fear in the judgment. In fact, God established the judgment to determine who are willing to be forgiven. As Romans puts it, *there is "no condemnation to those who are in Christ Jesus"* (Romans 8:1; emphasis added).

That is very good news!

- The good news is that the Judge is on our side.
- The good news is that the Judge sent the Savior.
- The good news is that all who have accepted Jesus' life and death are safe in Him.
- The good news is that the purpose of the judgment is the vindication of God's people.

Praise God for the resurrected Jesus, who is now representing each of His children in the heavenly temple above! Praise God that Jesus will return to take His faithful ones to heaven! Praise God that the judgment is good news!

18

The Hope of the World

For the grace of God has appeared for the salvation of all men, training us to renounce irreligion and worldly passions, and to live sober, upright, and godly lives in this world, awaiting our blessed hope, the appearing of the glory of our great God and Savior Jesus Christ, who gave himself for us to redeem us from all iniquity and to purify for himself a people of his own who are zealous for good deeds.
—Titus 2:11–14, RSV

Hope is the central word in any discussion of the return of Jesus.

All we have to do is read the daily newspaper or watch the evening news to realize that the world is messed up along with the people in it. And if that isn't enough to depress you, try meditating upon the end of your life. Whether you like it or not, your end will be either death by sickness or death by violent accident. Not much to look forward to there. That is why Paul characterized those who had no faith in Christ as those who "have no hope" (1 Thessalonians 4:13).

It is in the context of that "no hope" passage that

Paul makes his most complete presentation of the return of Jesus at the end of human history (1 Thessalonians 4:13–15:11). In another connection, the apostle refers to the Second Advent as the "blessed hope" (Titus 2:13). It is a blessed event because it puts an end to the hopelessness of a sick world that moves from one disaster to another—and replaces it with a re-created "new earth" in which there will be no more tears, death, sorrow, or pain, "for the former things have passed away" (Revelation 21:4).

Jesus Himself set the stage for our study of His return to Earth at the end of Earth's history. "Let not your heart be troubled," He told His disciples on the eve of His crucifixion, "you believe in God, believe also in Me. In My Father's house are many mansions; if it were not so, I would have told you. I go to prepare a place for you. And if I go and prepare a place for you, *I will come again* and receive you to Myself; that where I am, there you may be also" (John 14:1–3; emphasis added). Jesus' fullest presentation on the topic is His great sermon on the Second Advent, found in Matthew 24 and 25.

The fact of His second coming is one of the most widespread teachings in the New Testament. The good news is that the Bible not only highlights the reality of the event but also how it will take place.

An anything-but-secret return
One can only wonder how the teachings of the secret

The Hope of the World

rapture and a secret return of Jesus ever got started. The Bible sets forth the second coming of Jesus as the most public event of world history.

Jesus set the stage when He told His disciples that "as the lightning comes from the east and flashes to the west, so also will the coming of the Son of Man be" (Matthew 24:27). The book of Revelation builds upon that claim when it reports that "He is coming with clouds, and every eye will see Him" (Revelation 1:7). That is hardly a secret return.

It is clear that the Second Advent will be the worst-kept secret in history. But what about the rapture? Couldn't it be secret? Not according to the Bible.

The Bible's most vivid description of the rapture is in 1 Thessalonians 4, in which Paul writes that when Christ returns "we who are alive and remain shall be *caught up* together with them [the resurrected dead] in the clouds to meet the Lord in the air" (verse 17; emphasis added). The words to notice in that verse are "caught up." The Greek word behind that translation means to "seize," to "snatch away," and to "transport hastily." It has worked its way into English as "rapture" through the Latin *rapio*. So when Paul speaks of the end-time rapture, he means the event in which God's people are "caught up" or raptured at the Second Advent to meet Jesus who is coming in the clouds of heaven.

And just how secret is that rapture? Let's let Paul

supply us with the Bible's answer. In the verse right before his discussion of the saints being "caught up," he writes that "the Lord Himself will descend from heaven with a shout, with the voice of an archangel, and with the trumpet of God" (1 Thessalonians 4:16).

The apostle presents a similar picture in 1 Corinthians, in which he writes: "Behold, I tell you a mystery: We shall not all sleep [die], but we shall all be changed—in a moment, in the twinkling of an eye, at the last trumpet. For the trumpet will sound, and the dead will be raised incorruptible, and we shall be changed" (1 Corinthians 15:51, 52).

In summary, the anything-but-secret rapture will be accompanied by the following:

1. A massive shout (1 Thessalonians 4:16)
2. The voice of an archangel (verse 16)
3. The blaring of a trumpet (verse 16; 1 Corinthians 15:52)
4. A heavenly display that will be as visible as lightning that illuminates the sky from east to west (Matthew 24:27)
5. A visibility so widespread that every eye will see it (Revelation 1:7)
6. Around the entire world, the opening up of the graves and the resurrection of the dead who have accepted Jesus as their Lord (1 Thessalonians 4:16; 1 Corinthians 15:52)

The actual facts of the Second Advent and the simultaneous rapture (or catching up) of the saints will be the most visible and audible event in world history.

Hope for you and me

I don't know about you, but I get discouraged from time to time. And I know that I am not alone. Even Jesus' disciples got weighed down with the discouraging events they had to face. It is no accident that He said to them right before the cross that they were not to let their hearts be troubled because He was only leaving them so that He could go to heaven and prepare a place for them so He could return and take them home to be with Him (John 14:1–3).

In that promise, there is hope for all of us. The "blessed hope" of the ages is the return of our Lord Jesus in the clouds. At that time, the dead who have accepted Christ will be resurrected, while living Christians will be caught up (or raptured) to meet both Jesus and the resurrected believers in the air. And all of that will be in the celebratory environment of blaring trumpets and shouts of joy and victory filling the air.

I want to be there on that day. I want to not only see Jesus coming in the clouds with all of His angels—but I want to be with Him through all eternity. And I want you, dear friend, to join me at the party.

19

Being Ready to Meet Jesus

"Watch out, then, because you do not know what day your Lord will come. If the owner of a house knew the time when the thief would come, you can be sure that he would stay awake and not let the thief break into his house. So then, you also must always be ready, because the Son of Man will come at an hour when you are not expecting him."
—Matthew 24:42–44, GNT

In a previous chapter, we examined the certainty of the return of Jesus. In this one, we want to look at what the Bible says about being ready for the most important event in the history of the world.

The focus of Jesus

Curiously, Jesus was more interested in telling His first disciples (and us) how to be ready for the Second Advent than about its timing. Of course, in His great sermon on the Second Coming in Matthew 24 and 25, He did provide some signs. But interestingly enough, there have been wars, rumors of wars, earthquakes, and famines in every generation. As a result, He told them that such signs were not the end (Matthew 24:6) but rather "the beginning of sorrows" (verse 8). It is as if He were saying, every time you see these things remember that you live in a sick world and that I will return to rescue you out of it. But while the signs in Matthew 24:3–8 are not all that specific, they do keep the topic in our minds as we take in the daily news.

A much more specific sign of nearness, and one that can have only one possible fulfillment is found in verse 14, in which Jesus tells us that "this gospel of the kingdom will be preached in all the world as a witness to all the nations, and then the end will come." With the rise of modern missions, and especially with the development of ever more powerful means of communication, the fulfillment of that commission is for the first time in history a genuine possibility.

Of course, there are also signs of Jesus' return in the social world as sin continues to pervert human values (2 Timothy 3:1–6). However, some of these signs of the nearness of the end in the social realm are not even mentioned as such in the Bible. But such issues as nuclear proliferation and the side effects on the environment from overpopulation and global warming also make the continuing existence of world civilization questionable. As some social and physical scientists see it, the question is not *if* humankind will destroy the planet but *when*. All we know for sure is that Jesus will return before that time; at His return, He will "destroy those who" would "destroy the earth" (Revelation 11:18).

The only thing Jesus actually called a "sign" in Matthew 24 was at His advent: "Then the sign of the Son of Man will appear in heaven, . . . and they will see the Son of Man coming on the clouds of heaven with power and great glory" (verse 30). That is not a sign of nearness but of the reality that the Second Advent is taking place. That thought lines up with the fact that both Jesus and Paul taught that the Second Coming would come like "a thief in the night" and catch most people off guard (1 Thessalonians 5:2; cf. Matthew 24:42–44).

But Jesus and Paul emphasized the fact that no Christian need be caught off guard (1 Thessalonians 5:4). It is for that reason that Jesus' major presentation on His return climaxes with five parables emphasizing the need for His followers to watch and be ready. That is what our Lord saw as the greatest need of His church between His ascension to heaven and His second advent.

How to be ready

The first of Christ's parables on readiness for His return is found in Matthew 24:43, in which He tells us to watch since we do not know exactly when He will return. He completes that thought with the idea that

He would be "coming at an hour you do not expect" (verse 44). The least expected time, of course, is today. But some *today* He will fulfill His promise and catch those off guard who are waiting for *tomorrow*.

That thought brings to my mind the fable of three apprentice devils, who were being sent to Earth to complete their training. Each presented his plan to Satan for the ruination of humanity. The first proposed to tell people that there is no God. Satan replied that this plan would not delude many, since most have a gut feeling to the contrary. The second said he would proclaim that there was no hell. Satan rejected this tactic also, since most people have a sense that sin will receive its just reward. "The third said: 'I will tell them there is no hurry.' 'Go,' said Satan, 'and you will ruin them by the thousand.' "[1]

The most dangerous delusion in our day is that time will go on indefinitely. That is the devil's theology. Christ has told us that earthly history will indeed come to an end. Each of us must choose which one to believe.

The second parable in Matthew 24 (verses 45–51) continues Christ's emphasis on waiting. But it adds that His second coming would be delayed, and because of the delay, many would conclude that they didn't have to be faithful in their daily living and how they treated others. Such individuals would be surprised and would receive the reward of the wicked, even though outwardly they were His followers.

The third parable (Matthew 25:1–13) carries on the theme of waiting in watchful expectation but emphasizes that each of us must personally be ready for His return as the Bridegroom. There will be no time to get ready after He has arrived. Now is the time to prepare.

The fourth parable (verses 14–30) continues the previous emphases, including the fact that Jesus would be away "a long time" (verse 19), but adds that while faithfully watching, it is also necessary to work and increase the gifts or talents that God has entrusted to each of His followers.

The final parable (verses 31–46) deals with the end-time judgment of the sheep and the goats and highlights the kind of work His followers are to do while waiting and watching—namely, to share God's love in caring for the needy and neglected of the earth.

Peter's appeal

The apostle Peter writes that in the last days scoffers will arise, telling us that the return of Jesus is a delusion; that all things are continuing as they always have (2 Peter 3:3, 4).

But he retorts, "The Lord is not slack concerning His promise" (verse 9). "The day of the Lord will come as a thief. . . . Therefore, since all these things will be dissolved, what manner of persons ought you to be in holy conduct and godliness?" (verses 10, 11).

Good question. It is one that each of us must answer for our self.

---

1. William Barclay, *The Gospel of Matthew*, vol. 2, New Daily Study Bible (Louisville, KY: Westminster John Knox, 2001), 370.

20

What Happens After Jesus Returns?

> *Then I saw an angel coming down from heaven, having the key to the bottomless pit and a great chain in his hand. He laid hold of the dragon, that serpent of old, who is the Devil and Satan, and bound him for a thousand years . . . so that he should deceive the nations no more till the thousand years were finished.*
> —Revelation 20:1–3

The climax of earthly history is described in Revelation 19, which vividly portrays Jesus' second coming. *That is clear enough*, you may be thinking, *but what happens after Jesus returns?*

The answer to that question is the topic of Revelation 20, which discusses the time period that Christians call the *millennium* (a term derived from two Latin words meaning "thousand" and "years"). At the end of that thousand-year period, Revelation 21 tells us, God creates a new earth in which there is no more sin or sorrow. Thus the millennium spans the thousand years between the second coming of Jesus and the

What Happens After Jesus Returns?

re-creation of the earth as the eternal home of those saved by God's grace.

That is understandable, but why is the millennial period even necessary? Why don't the saved go to their eternal home immediately?

Good questions. The best way to answer them is to examine the events that take place in connection with the millennium.

Millennial events

The Bible is clear that the millennium begins at the return of Jesus at the end of earthly history (Revelation 19:11–21). At that time, Christ's followers are resurrected and taken to heaven (1 Thessalonians 4:16, 17; Revelation 20:4, 6; John 14:1–3). At the same time, the earth is desolated and the wicked die (Revelation 18; 19:11–21; 20:5; 2 Thessalonians 1:7, 8). That leaves Satan bound on a ruined earth with no one to tempt (Revelation 20:1–3).

During the millennium, Scripture describes God's followers reigning with Christ in heaven (verses 4, 6). They are portrayed as sitting in judgment (Revelation 20:4; 1 Corinthians 6:2, 3). Meanwhile, as mentioned above, the earth is pictured as desolate, like the bottomless pit (Revelation 20:1–3), the wicked are in their graves (verse 5), and Satan is confined to the ruined earth with no humans to deceive.

At the end of the thousand years, the Bible tells us

that the wicked will be resurrected (verse 5). With that event, "Satan [is] . . . released from his prison and will go out to deceive the nations" once again (verses 7, 8). At the same time, the New Jerusalem descends from heaven with Christ and His saints (Revelation 21:2); Satan and his followers attack the holy city (Revelation 20:7–9), and they are eternally destroyed (what the Bible calls the "second death"; see verse 6) by God in the lake of fire (verses 11–15; 2 Peter 3:12). Then God forms "a new earth in which righteousness dwells" (2 Peter 3:13; cf. Revelation 21:1–5).

The *When* of the Millennium

The following time line indicates the place of the thousand-year period known as the millennium in the flow of the book of Revelation:

1. Last days of temporal history Revelation 12:17–19:10	3. Millennium Revelation 20
2. Second Coming Revelation 19:11–21	4. Eternity Revelation 21, 22

The purpose of the millennium

With the flow of biblical history in mind, we are now in position to deal with the function of the millennium in God's struggle with evil.

The key millennial purpose is found in Revelation 20:4, "And I saw thrones, and they sat on them, and judgment was committed to them." In short, the redeemed of all ages will be sitting in judgment. That thought is reflected upon by Paul, who asserts that "the saints will judge the world." They will even "judge angels" (1 Corinthians 6:2, 3).

Here we find a problem. What is the function of the millennial judgment? What remains to be judged? After all, the saints have already been determined worthy to come up in the first resurrection, and the wicked have obviously been found to be unworthy, since they are in their graves and will not rise until the second resurrection at the end of the thousand years.

One point is clear. The judgment of Revelation 20 is obviously not to see who is saved or lost. The pre-Advent judgment will have already made those decisions. And at the Second Advent, all will have received their just rewards.

But were the rewards actually just? Did God really do the right thing in saving some who had sinned, while condemning others who are awaiting the second resurrection?

Those are not questions for God to judge. But they are important questions.

Just think about it for a moment. What if your "saintly" old grandmother did not come up in the first resurrection? And what happened to your pastor, whose messages came right from the heart of the gospel? Why are they still in their graves?

On the other hand, there will be some people who come up in the first resurrection who you think should not be there. The thief who died on a cross with Jesus is a case in point. Most people knew him as a cutthroat and robber. He even cursed Christ while they both suffered in agony. How could he possibly be among the saved? If you were not aware of his last-minute, deathbed confession, you could never answer that question satisfactorily.

In short, if all have sinned and eternal death is the just reward for sinners (Romans 3:23; 6:23), then how could God save some while destroying others? Did He make the right decisions? On what basis? Can His judgments even be trusted?

That is what the millennial judgment is all about. It is the universe's judgment of God, based on the record "books" of heaven (Revelation 20:12). It is what might be called a *review judgment* by the righteous on God's actions in saving some while destroying others for eternity. We should never forget that the theme of the great songs of the book of Revelation focuses on the justice of God in His judgments (Revelation 15:3, 4; 16:5–7; 19:1, 2). That is the major issue of the ages. Can He be trusted?

And that is a crucial question because at the close of the millennium Satan and all the wicked will finally and forever be destroyed. Since that destruction is irreversible, God wants to make sure before it takes place that everyone is satisfied that He is doing the best thing. Only when that has been demonstrated to the satisfaction of all in the millennial judgment will the universe be secure for eternity.

At the end of the millennium, the whole universe will be able to sing with one accord that "salvation and glory and honor and power belong to the Lord our God! For true and righteous are His judgments" (Revelation 19:1, 2).

21

Infinite Hitler or Loving God?

The LORD Almighty says, "The day is coming when all proud and evil people will burn like straw. On that day they will burn up, and there will be nothing left of them."
—Malachi 4:1, GNT

Auschwitz, Dachau, Buchenwald—horrid symbols burned into the world's memory.*

What do these extermination camps for millions of people bring to mind? Adolf Hitler's "final solution" to rid the earth of the "Jewish problem." They are symbols of a world gone wrong. Coupled with the prolonged use of torture, they represent the apex of humanity's cruelty toward its own kind.

The best that can be said of them is that their victims eventually died. Even though mid-twentieth century totalitarian regimes had honed to a fine "science" the ability to keep certain interrogation subjects alive for the longest time possible to extract maximum

---

* Portions of this chapter were previously published in the March 2014 issue of *Signs of the Times*®.

Infinite Hitler or Loving God?

information from them, their bodies finally gave up, and they ceased to exist.

Torture without end

Yet many Christians hold a view of God that makes Him infinitely more diabolical than these totalitarian forces. The traditional doctrine of hell advances that view. Reading Bible texts that talk of the "lake of fire" (Revelation 20:14), "everlasting punishment" (Matthew 25:46), "unquenchable fire" (Matthew 3:12), "everlasting fire" (Matthew 25:41), and "eternal condemnation" (Mark 3:29), many have concluded that the wicked face an endless burning in hell throughout the ceaseless ages of eternity.

One nineteenth-century children's storybook illustrates this idea vividly for its tender audience. In addition to presenting several graphic stories of children suffering in various forms of never-ending fire, it seeks to show just how nasty forever would be in such an environment. "Little child," we read, "if you go to Hell, there will be a devil at your side to strike you. He will go on striking you every minute for ever and ever, without ever stopping." The first blow will create sores worse than those of Job; the second will double the affliction, and so on. "How then will your body be, after the devil has been striking it every moment for a hundred million of years without stopping?"[1]

Variations on such themes have been used by hellfire

117

preachers for centuries. Of course, the traditional view of hell has some obvious problems. After all, everyone knows that real bodies in real fire eventually burn up. Augustine, the church's most influential thinker for more than a thousand years, had the answer to that dilemma. He assured his readers that God will employ His miracle-working power to keep sinners alive and conscious in those never-ending torments.

As might be expected, such open talk of hellfire has not been popular in the past hundred years. Influential Roman Catholic theologian Hans Küng put his finger on the key issue for the topic's unpopularity when he asked: "What would we think of a human being who satisfied his thirst for revenge so implacably and insatiably?" In the next passage, he goes on to note that "the idea not only of a lifelong, but even eternal punishment of body and soul, seems to many people absolutely monstrous."[2]

British Protestant theologian John Wenham agrees. "I believe," he writes, "that endless torment is a hideous and unscriptural doctrine which has been a terrible burden on the mind of the church for many centuries and a terrible blot on her presentation of the gospel."[3]

The Bible on hell

The good news is that the Bible pictures the eternal fate of the wicked as death rather than everlasting suffering. So we read in Romans that "the wages of sin is *death*, but the gift of God is eternal life in Christ Jesus our Lord" (Romans 6:23; emphasis added). One wonders how people can read such a clear passage and interpret the future of the wicked in terms of endless, conscious suffering rather than death.

And that passage doesn't stand alone. Revelation 20:9 tells us that the fire God sends to purify the earth *devours* the wicked. Psalm 37:20 says they will *perish*. And Paul tells us they will be *destroyed* (Philippians 3:19). Malachi adds that "the day which is coming shall burn them up" (Malachi 4:1).

Jesus presents the same picture. Not only does He tell us that the wicked will be burned up just like weeds thrown into fire (Matthew 13:40, 42, 49, 50) but also that both their souls and bodies will be destroyed in hell (Matthew 10:28). In Revelation, this final destruction of the wicked is called the "second death" (Revelation 21:8).

But, you may be thinking, *if the Bible is so plain on the topic, how did so many people become confused?* The first part of the answer is Satan's great lie in Eden. God had told Adam and Eve that they would "surely die" if they sinned (Genesis 2:17). The devil contradicted God, saying that they wouldn't die—thereby inferring that sinners would exist eternally (Genesis 3:4).

Once Satan had misled the bulk of the human race on the future state of the wicked, he could get them to overlook such texts as 1 Timothy 6:15, 16, which clearly states that only God has immortality; 2 Timothy 1:10, which teaches that humans gain immortality through accepting Jesus; and 1 Corinthians 15:50–54, which says that the gift of immortality is not granted even to Christians until the second coming of Jesus.

Because the wicked never accept Jesus, they will never be granted immortality. Thus they are subject to death and cannot live forever.

Another look at "forever"
That last point raises yet another question: What does the Bible mean when it says that the wicked will suffer "eternal condemnation," "everlasting fire," and "everlasting punishment" in "unquenchable fire"?

First, we should note that in the Bible "eternal" refers to *eternal results* rather than an endless process. An illustration of this fact is that Jude 7 tells us Sodom and Gomorrah are suffering the vengeance of "eternal fire." Yet they are not still burning. They burned up and were destroyed. Similarly, "forever" is also a limited term. Thus a slave could serve his or her master "forever" (Exodus 21:6), obviously meaning until death.

It is little wonder that hellfire is described as the "second death" (Revelation 21:8). God is no infinite Hitler. Rather, in His love, He does the very best thing in a bad situation. He allows the wicked to rest in everlasting death.

Infinite Hitler or Loving God?

But that is only half of the story. The best part of the God of love is that even though "the wages of sin is death, ... the gift of God is eternal life in Christ Jesus" (Romans 6:23).

---

1. John Furniss, *The Sight of Hell* (Dublin: James Duffy, 1874), 13, 14.

2. Hans Küng, *Eternal Life? Life After Death as a Medical, Philosophical, and Theological Problem*, trans. Edward Quinn (New York: Doubleday, 1984), 136, 137.

3. John Wenham, *Facing Hell: An Autobiography, 1913–1996* (Carlisle, UK: Paternoster, 1998), vii.

22

The Eternal Home of God's Children

*And I heard a loud voice from heaven saying,
"Behold, the tabernacle of God is with men,
and He will dwell with them. . . .
God Himself will be with them and be their God.
And God will wipe away every tear from their eyes;
there shall be no more death, nor sorrow, nor crying.
There shall be no more pain,
for the former things have passed away."*
—Revelation 21:3, 4

Christians have had an interest in heaven since the time of Jesus—and for good reason. Part of His final instruction to His disciples before the cross was that He was going to His Father in heaven and would return for them after He had prepared them a place (John 14:1–3).

That theme is picked up by Paul, who tells us that when Jesus returns, both living believers and the resurrected dead will be caught up to meet Jesus in the air as the first portion of their trip to heaven (1 Thessalonians 4:16, 17).

The Eternal Home of God's Children

The new earth

One interesting fact about the stay of God's saints in heaven is that it lasts for only a thousand years. At the end of that millennial period, "the holy city, New Jerusalem," comes down "out of heaven from God" (Revelation 21:2, 10).

The Bible makes it plain that "the first [atmospheric] heaven and the first earth [the sick planet that we now dwell upon]" will pass away (verse 1) through the agency of the cleansing fire of what the book of Revelation calls the "lake of fire" (Revelation 20:10, 14). That fire will purge the earth of sin and its results (2 Peter 3:12). God will then create "a new earth in which righteousness dwells" (verse 13). It is this new earth that will be the home of the saved.

But, we need to ask, what will the new earth be like? The answer comes in two flavors: negative and positive descriptions.

The new earth—a negative perspective

The negative description is reflected upon by John the revelator. He tells us that "God will wipe away every tear from their eyes; there shall be no more death, nor sorrow, nor crying. There shall be no more pain, for the former things have passed away" (Revelation 21:4). John also notes that there will be "no more sea" (verse 1). Today the seas cover most of the earth. But in the new earth, they apparently will be much smaller, thereby providing more land for human usage. Along that line, other passages imply that there will be no more deserts (Isaiah 35:6, 7).

Why the negative in these descriptions? Because the human mind, with its limited experience, cannot even begin to grasp the glories of God's realm. They are beyond the scope of our thinking and thus impossible to describe to such limited beings.

On the other hand, we earthlings do know what we have to face on this earth and what we would like to escape from. As a result, we find Revelation telling us that there will be no more sorrow and death in the new earth, and even that there would be no massive oceans and deserts, thereby representing symbolically that the entire earth will be agriculturally fruitful. Thus there will be no more hunger.

The negatives are helpful and encouraging. But they provide only the slightest glimmer of what awaits those who choose to live with Jesus throughout infinite time. The good news is that God has revealed some positive aspects of the new earth to help fill out our understanding.

The new earth—a positive perspective

Eden restored is the best way to describe the re-created earth. Revelation tells us of "a pure river of water of life, clear as crystal, proceeding from the throne of God" and the restoration of "the tree of life" (Revelation 22:1,

2). Beyond that, Revelation reflects on the conditions of Eden when it tells us that there will be "no more curse"—referring to the deadly results of sin (verse 3).

But the best thing about the new earth will be the presence of Jesus Himself. He may be, in a spiritual sense, the light of our life during our present journey, but there His glory will literally be all the light we need (Revelation 21:22–25).

I have to admit that I do not fully understand such things. But I look forward to learning more about them.

We can be thankful that Isaiah presents us with a peek into the conditions on the new earth. His word pictures have been some of my favorites. Listen to the prophet:

> "The wolf also shall dwell with the lamb,
> The leopard shall lie down with the young goat,
> The calf and the young lion and the fatling together;
> And a little child shall lead them.
> The cow and the bear shall graze;
> Their young ones shall lie down together;
> And the lion shall eat straw like the ox. . . .
> They shall not hurt nor destroy in all My holy mountain,
> For the earth shall be full of the knowledge of the LORD
> As the waters cover the sea" (Isaiah 11:6, 7, 9).

God's Truth Can Change Your Life!

Again we read:

> Then the eyes of the blind shall be opened,
> And the ears of the deaf shall be unstopped.
> Then the lame shall leap like a deer,
> And the tongue of the dumb sing.
> For waters shall burst forth in the wilderness,
> And streams in the desert.
> The parched ground shall become a pool,
> And the thirsty land springs of water. . . .
>
> But the redeemed shall walk there,
> And the ransomed of the LORD shall return,
> And come to Zion with singing,
> With everlasting joy on their heads.
> They shall obtain joy and gladness,
> And sorrow and sighing shall flee away (Isaiah 35:5–7, 9, 10).

In another place, the prophet presents a picture of security and well-being when he writes:

> "They shall build houses and inhabit them;
> They shall plant vineyards and eat their fruit.
> They shall not build and another inhabit;
> They shall not plant and another eat;
> For . . . , My elect shall long enjoy the work of their hands" (Isaiah 65:21, 22).

And as in the book of Revelation, Isaiah tells us that the new earth will be Eden restored. In particular, he highlights the seventh-day Sabbath of Creation when "all flesh shall come to worship before" God (Isaiah 66:23). As on this present earth, fellowshiping with God on His holy day will be a special blessing.

Just reading about the home of the saved in the earth made new makes me excited to be there. I want to spend eternity with my Lord and Savior.

If you feel like me, why don't we just bow our heads right now and rededicate our lives and all that we have to that God who loved us so much that He sent His Son that we might have life eternal?

FREE Lessons at www.BibleStudies.com

Call:
1-888-456-7933

Write:
Discover
P.O. Box 999
Loveland, CO 80539-0999

It's easy to learn more about the Bible!